Also by NORMAN HARPER

First Daily

Spik o the Place

Stronach Vol I

Stronach Vol II

Stronach Vol III

The Stronach Tapes

Weeks in the Howe

A Dash o Doric
(with Robbie Shepherd)

Anither Dash o Doric
(with Robbie Shepherd)

Fortnights

Norman Harper

Aberdeen Journals Ltd

First published in 2001 by
ABERDEEN JOURNALS LTD
Mastrick, Aberdeen, Scotland AB15 6DF

Cover artwork of The Fountain, Alford,
and cover design by Susan Bell

British Library Cataloguing-in-publication data
A catalogue record for this volume
is available on request

ISBN 1 901300 08 0

Printed in Scotland by Polestar AUP Aberdeen Ltd.

For Cameron and Nicholas

Contents

— — — —

Foreword

by Phyllis Walker

(Norman's teacher in Primary Six and Primary Seven)

ONE day, a 10-year-old boy approached me in the classroom and asked: "Do you think I could start a class newspaper?" It was very unusual for 10-year-old pupils to volunteer to do extra written work, and especially unusual for 10-year-old boys, but you'll have guessed already that the boy was Norman just over 30 years ago.

I don't remember my exact words, but the gist of the reply was: "Yes, but you'll have to organise it and persuade the rest of the class to help you with the work, and mostly in your own time." I might have added that I knew little about newspapers myself, but I left it at that.

The 11+ exams were still with us at that time, and although we were not allowed to practise any of the tests involved, I thought it my duty to ensure that all pupils were as proficient as possible in the three Rs, so there was very little time for "extras".

We did, of course, have much written work to cover: projects in history, geography and nature study. We had an Aberdeenshire Education Authority scheme of work to follow.

So Norman went off and in no time at all he appeared with his list of helpers. He had recruited:

1. Serial story writers, each one briefed to structure the writing in such a way that every episode ended with a cliffhanger to keep the readers coming back, of course.

2. A writer and co-ordinator for the joke page.

3. An artist to draw pictures for the strip cartoons.

4. An organiser to deal with the letters to the editor (the editor being Norman himself, naturally).

5. A persuasive person to prise interesting items of news from pupils not so much involved as the team.

Norman was fortunate that there were many other gifted pupils in that class, so they set about their tasks with a will. I know this only because of the results, as I took little or no part in the organising of the paper. Much of their work was done during morning intervals and lunch breaks.

Only the pupils involved will know how much argument or discussion there was about a name for the newspaper, but the two on the short list were Story Weekly and The Orbit. I imagined that The Orbit was going to be a clear winner, because space travel was very new and of much interest to children at this time. In fact, they picked Story Weekly.

Unfortunately, we had no copying facilities in the school, even in the secondary department, so each newspaper had to be handwritten, and only one copy every week was produced. Sometimes, they missed edition deadline, to Norman's great distress. Maybe the joke page was not complete or maybe one of the serial writers was off ill, but eventually each new issue appeared and was much sought after by the pupils.

The Letters to the Editor page was very interesting, informative and highly amusing. I doubt if Norman realised this, but sometimes I took a copy to the staffroom and we were very impressed with the editor's skills in handling his readers' comments or complaints.

Sometimes a litter was not too complimentary: the jokes were old, the stories were boring, and so on. How was an editor to respond to such criticism? One wrong word and he might lose a writer or an artist. The editor had to be very diplomatic with his replies, and I don't remember any of his staff resigning in a huff.

A competition page was introduced at one point and prizes had to be awarded. Norman reminded me of this just a few years ago.

He said I had given him half a crown (12.5p) and that he had bought 10 bags of crisps for the winners. I doubt if today's children would be pleased with such a prize, but I'm sure that the Story Weekly readers were quite chuffed.

So the copies kept coming. New ideas were introduced and Story Weekly's popularity might have been assessed by the somewhat tattery condition of each issue after a few days. Children were allowed to take the one and only copy home if they wished. By the time 40 pupils had thumbed their way through the handwritten pages, and then the same had been done by brothers and sisters and maybe parents at home, you can imagine the state of the newspaper.

As far as I know, not one copy of Story Weekly exists. Several students, teachers or would-be journalists have contacted me, hoping that I might have some of Norman's early work in my possession. Unfortunately, the answer is No. Story Weekly's pages were so grimy by the time the succeeding issue appeared that old copies ended up in the bin.

Other project work and stories always went home at the end of each term. I often wish that I had kept back one or two of Norman's imaginative and fun-filled tales. Children love to hear stories written by their own age group.

Norman must have had a feeling — an inclination — for journalism before he became a Primary Six pupil, as it was wholly his suggestion to start the class newspaper. He must have studied the Press and Journal and other papers as he had so many ideas to share with his classmates.

And what influence had he on some of these classmates? We'll never know for sure, but I understand that at least one other pupil, and perhaps two, from that same class made journalism their chosen professions. Three journalists from one class in a village school! That must be unusual, surely.

So, now you know how and when Norman's journalistic career started. Many people over the years have asked me if I had known Norman when he was a schoolboy, so I thought this foreword was at last a golden opportunity to tell how it was.

I'm sure you'll enjoy this latest collection of Norman's

Introduction

by Norman Harper

PROBABLY the most difficult thing about writing a sequel book is the thing that most people would think was the easiest: finding a title. Since Weeks in the Howe's appearance two years ago, we've been planning idly for a second outing and the volume you're holding is the result.

One of the last decisions to be made, however, was what this book would be called. I didn't want to follow the standard format and call it More Weeks in the Howe or Back in the Howe Again. Neither did I want to abandon the Howe theme entirely.

So I cast about among colleagues and family for ideas and Fortnights is the result. Why Fortnights? You'll forgive the tortured reasoning, but someone worked out that this was Volume Two of "Weeks" and two weeks is a fortnight. I hope she's not considering a career in stand-up comedy.

I'm delighted that the Fortnights foreword has been written by someone who had more influence on my choice of career than probably anyone else. Phyllis Walker was wise enough to see when someone was interested in a particular discipline, and bold enough to know how to engineer the time and guidance so that he could follow his instincts.

Indeed, my whole career is built on four happy coincidences. Miss McDonald, my teacher in Primary One and Two, had a ready supply ofbooks round the classroom which I found intriguing. Better still, she encouraged us to explore them.

In Primary Three we had the redoubtable Miss Alexander, very much a woman of the old school, who inspired not a little fear in her pupils, but who force-fed me the rules of grammar, spelling and punctuation which too few current pupils know or are prepared to learn. Sometimes, you wonder if some are aware that these even exist.

When I reached Primary Four and Five, I was in the capable hands of Jessie Stewart, just as much a stickler for accuracy but, from my perspective as an eight-year-old, with a much kindlier way about her. Most pupils in her class felt able to relax a little more. What tickled me most about her was that she had a twinkle in her eye and was not averse to seeing a little Doric in our English compositions. I well recall that she gave me an extra mark for the correct contextual use of the word galluses (braces) in a school essay, but then took the mark away again because I had mis-spelled it.

And then came Miss Walker, who took everything I had learned in the previous five years, polished me up substantially and gave me enough rope to see what pleasure there could be in playing around with the English language.

What you have here are 52 examples of my playing around with the English language during my more recent years at the Press and Journal. Once again, they're in no particular order and, once again, I hope you enjoy your book.

Norman Harper
The Howe
October, 2001

The
Columns

1. AND NOW, A WEATHER REPORT

Or why rain, sun and blin drift will always fascinate us

■■■ ■■■ ■■ ■■

"They say the English are obsessed with the weather,
but it's almost a religion up with you." He was right,
but it's a religion born of necessity.

IT MUST have been an interesting introduction to life in northern Scotland for the young Met Office forecaster. He had arrived from somewhere in the Home Counties to take up his Aberdeen posting in December, 1978. Either on his first or second morning, he had lifted the phone to hear a broad Buchan accent on the other end of the line.

"Is aat the Met Office?"

"It is."

"Are ee a forecaaster?"

"I am."

"Fine. I jist wintit tae tell ye I've spent the last three oors shovellin twa fit o 'partly cloudy' aff ma fairm road."

The young forecaster was able to laugh about it 15 years later, when he was a senior man in Glasgow, but at the time he regarded it as a baptism of fire. "They say the English are obsessed by the weather," he told me, "but it's almost a religion up with you."

He was right, but it's a religion born of necessity. More than in most parts of the country, our forefathers were compelled to take an interest in the weather, for the weather meant the difference between a comfortable living or penury. In many cases, it was literally the difference between life and death. Farming and fishing, the two native industries throughout the millennium, were, are and always will be governed by the weather, hence our healthy crop of weather lore. Try these:

If the cock craws at nicht, he'll rise wi a watery heid.
Lang fair, lang fool.
A green Yule maks a fat kirkyaird.

Many of northern Scotland's weather sayings are in rhyme:

A blast fae the west is a blast at the maist,
bit a blast fae the east is three days at least.

Fin Bennachie pits on its cap,
the Garioch lads'll get a drap.

If November ice can haud a duck,
the rest o the winter's dubs and muck.

And sometimes the richness of description of the weather knocks standard English into a cocket hat:

The dreep at the eyn o ma nose wid droon a cat.

Notice how all of these examples labour bad weather. I can't think of more than half a dozen sayings relating to sunny days, because weather lore had a purpose. It foretold bad weather so that fishers could batten down the hatches and farmers could bolt the barn doors. There was nothing to fear in good weather, so no need to warn of it.

How accurate were these sayings? You'd be surprised. You'll find many pensioners, even now, who prefer to glance at the trees, clouds, birds and beasts for their personal forecast each evening and morning, rather than relying on Heather with the Weather.

I well recall a wedding of a young woman from Glenkindie, in Upper Donside. As the wedding week dawned, the long-range professional forecast for farmers, broadcast on the BBC each

Sunday, had warned of the foulest weather for the foreseeable future. Like all brides-to-be, the young woman had been distraught. Her father (we'll call him Geordie), a farmer in his late 50s at the time, had cautioned calm because he was certain that she was worrying needlessly. She had to trust him, he said.

Geordie's daughter knew that her father believed deeply in the lore of his ancestors, but she knew equally that he would have said anything to lift her spirits.

By Thursday, the weather had been worsening steadily for four days, with not even a blink of sun. The rivers and burns, as we say, were lippin fu.

On the Friday, with flood warnings on roads everywhere from Inverness to Laurencekirk, and even some serious talk of a new Moray spate, the bride-to-be had almost resigned herself to a wedding in driving rain and roads turned into rivers. Her father remained confident that Saturday would smile kindly on her.

And now you want me to tell you that he was right all along.

Well, Geordie was more right than wrong; let's say that. Nobody could have claimed that the wedding Saturday was a July day that would have pleased tourists and made farmers grin, but the clouds rolled back for long enough to let bride and groom stay dry.

When I asked Geordie later why he had been so confident, he just smiled and said: "Misty Mey and dreepin Jeen, syne gweed weather fin that's deen."

Then, as he turned to go, he added: "Gey close, though."

Just by the way, Geordie was noted throughout Donside for his twinkling sense of humour. He had kidded his daughter that he was alarmed by the cost of a white wedding and that it would very likely bankrupt him. Seeing her chances of her big day evaporating, she had pointed out that surely he wouldn't want to see his only daughter married in a registrar's office.

"Meet me half-wye," he had said. "We'll pent the shotgun fite."

This dry humour must have run in the family, for it was Geordie's farmer brother, Wullie, who was heard once in the village shop complaining that the weather was so frosty that "ma hens is layin eggs stannin up".

He was also said to have been responsible — although I can't rely on my source — for noting that it had been so cold over one February night that he had fallen out of bed "and crackit ma long-johns".

Another evening, supposedly, his teeth had been chattering all night. When another customer at the bar had suggested that there was nothing unusual in that, Wullie had said: "They were in a gless aside ma bed."

But for true insight into the sanguine attitude we have to the weather in northern Scotland, come with me to a bus shelter at Cruden Bay, where two elderly ladies are sitting waiting for transport to Aberdeen. I can vouch for the truth of this, for the third occupant was an impeccably reliable source.

It was another day of driving rain. The water was spattering and splattering off the sides of the shelter, and the wind driving round the women's feet fit to soak them.

After five minutes' chatter and a few minutes silence, one of the women peered outside and saw only a thick mat of black, angry clouds in all directions. She sat back, turned to her companion and said: "I dinna think the sun's comin oot the day."

Her companion sniffed.

"Well," she said, "only feels and bairns wid come oot on a day like this."

━━ ━━ ━━ ━━

This column appeared in a special supplement in the Press and Journal in 1999 which was designed to explain the real northern Scotland to potential tourists and other visitors.

It drew several complaints from tourist bodies who deplored the fact that I had mentioned that we sometimes suffered bad weather.

One wonders what planet these people inhabit.

2. SAVOURING THE STAFF OF LIFE

Or why man can live perfectly well without tomato herb bread

■■ ■■ ■■ ■■

*"Until you've tried a breadmaking machine, it is difficult
to understand how foolproof the results can be. The
novelty of 100% success can be seductive."*

IT HAS been a uberous week in the howe. Everyone in the
country is more than a week into their new-century fitness
programmes (you are, aren't you?). We can see queues of
joggers passing the front of our house at the weekends. If we go
for a walk in the village, there's the tell-tale thump-click thump-
click thump-click of skipping-ropes on garage floors. The doors of
the howe swimming pool are being battered every morning by
customers anxious to shed those festive pounds. Ghostly blue
glows of home-tanning units shine from assorted bedroom
windows.

Well, not in this abode.

Here, we can't get moved for bread. Yes, bread.

We can trace the origins of this week's lament to early
December when, devoid of inspiration, I did something I have not
done in eight years of marriage: I asked Mrs Harper what she
would like as a festive present.

Having plied her with pendants and bracelets, frocks and
scarves for almost as long as I can remember, all of them received
with unbridled delight, I may add, I felt it was time that she had
more of a say in the selection of her end-of-year trinket.

Had she said: "Och, I don't know; surprise me", I would have locked her in the coalshed. As it was, she said: "Oh, something personal would be nice." But after eight years of something personal, that didn't get me any farther along the road.

So I gave her one of those bread-making machines. From the sensible, masculine point of view, this fulfilled four criteria: it was functional, it was productive, it was likely to recoup its own cost in time and she likes cooking.

Women readers, and perhaps a few men, are now appalled that anyone should select his wife's gift in so calculated a manner. A few of you have decided already that I deserved to have the thing broken over my head.

I'm sorry to disappoint you, but she was ecstatic. Truly. She had had a notion for a bread machine since seeing them road-tested on some BBC consumer programme a couple of years back. Besides, she has never really shared my taste for 12p cotton-wool loaves from supermarkets.

Since Hogmanay, rarely has the machine had a day to itself. It churns out loaves through the day. It is programmed to churn out loaves through the night. I go to sleep to the steady whirr of dough being kneaded in the larder downstairs. I rise to the yeasty smell of fresh-baked bread in the mornings.

All of this is most pleasant, and one of those machines certainly weans you off plastic-bag bread. I wouldn't say the results are cheap, but it works out at much the same cost as premium breads and production is so easy that it can become habit-forming.

The trouble is that there are only the two of us in this house (three if you count the dog), and we have not a hope of getting through all this bread.

Rapidly, we are coming to the stage when one of three things will have to happen: we will have to buy another freezer; we will have to sign up as sub-contractors to Sunblest, or I will have to remove the fuse from the plug and pretend that the machine has been broken beyond repair.

This is all a problem of success, I suppose. Until you've tried a bread-making machine, it is difficult to appreciate how foolproof it is and how good the results can be. Speaking as someone who, in the past, found home-made bread worthwhile only in that kneading the dough cleaned your hands, the novelty of 100% success each time, every time can be seductive.

Anyone who is sceptical of the theory that dumping half a dozen raw ingredients in an aluminium bucket can result, three hours later, in a perfectly risen and nicely golden loaf with the hand-made look and the home-made taste should think again.

The machine has turned out ordinary white bread, brown bread, wholemeal bread, tomato bread and herb bread. It has disgorged focaccia, ciabatta, pizza dough, brioche and croissants. We have an array of lemon loaves, cinnamon loaves, raisin loaves, cinnamon-and-raisin loaves and madeira cake.

Not one of them has been duff.

As a result, ours must be the only household in Scotland whose occupants have put on weight in the week after New Year. The robins and finches that were once happy to cock their heads and chirp on the bird table, now congregate round the back door in scenes that would inspire Hitchcock.

You can tell which of the howe's blackbirds have been dining Chez Harper: they're the ones that have to take a run before getting airborne.

But now that we have worked our way through the entire recipe book that came with the machine, with not a single omission along the way, I have ventured that the time has come for a temporary halt. Mrs Harper has agreed, albeit reluctantly.

If nothing else, there is a depressed look in the dog's eyes when he hauls himself out of his bed in the morning, stretches his legs, yawns, sniffs the air and looks up. It's a look that says: "Not again?"

I might also add that a diet which consists of so much bread, particularly the wholemeal variety, is not conducive to social decorum.

Which puts me in mind of a story that I read many years ago when I had an interest in the pre World War I monarchy. The story goes that King Edward VII's favourite black horse became so finicky in its dietary habits towards the end of its working life that the only food it would eat in any quantity was high-fibre black bread.

So fond of the horse was the king that he insisted that it be fed exactly what it wanted, no matter how inconvenient it might be to the royal household, or how difficult the logistics might be if the family happened to be out on tour.

Since the horse was also the king's favourite, it became a stalwart of royal ceremony. On one occasion, during a state visit of the German Kaiser, the horse was duly harnessed up with three others to haul the honoured guest, with the king, from Waterloo Station in procession to Buckingham Palace.

According to legend, as the king and kaiser alighted from the carriage in the palace courtyard, the horse shoogled a little on the cobbles and a loud report issued from its rear end, fluttering its tail in the process.

The king, a hearty chap with a robust sense of humour, grinned and beamed but, mindful of his cousin's dour nature, said: "I suppose I had better apologise for that."

"Think nothing of it," said the kaiser, "I'd just assumed it was the horse."

This column brought more reader response than any other that year; every correspondent wanting to know which particular make and model of machine we had bought.

To save the rest of you the price of a stamp, it was (and still is) a Prima 5 in stainless steel, although I believe it's also available in white plastic, which doesn't show buttery fingermarks quite so badly.

We've had only a couple of disasters in the two years since we began using it, both of which were blamed on me (naturally).

3. THE DUTCH CONNECTION

Or why you'd better not be fussed about food hygiene in Holland

▬ ▬ ▬ ▬

*"We watched the staff in one Dutch lunch cafe whack
out handfuls of boiled rice into takeaway containers.
Yes, handfuls. With their bare hands."*

IT HAS been an emetic week in the howe. You find me in something of a quandary this week, because there's something that I can't quite follow, despite the best efforts of scientific brains and statisticians to explain it to me.

We're just back from a pre-Easter break in Amsterdam and, yes, it was very pleasant, thank you very much for asking. It brought a whole new meaning to Mrs Harper's customary clarion when we are abroad: "They do so much more with their shop windows than we do at home."

I don't want to turn this into a What I Did On My Holidays essay, so I'll gloss over the Rijksmuseum and Rembrandtsplein, Keukenhof and Volendam, canal cruises and rijstafel, because many of you will know a lot more about those than I do, anyway.

Instead, answer me this. Is Scotland one of the most over-regulated countries on earth when it comes to health standards and food regulations? Of course it is. Pardon me for repeating the words of one irate shopkeeper in the howe, but you can hardly break wind in a shop nowadays without a mannie carrying a council clipboard appearing at your back to issue a written warning.

Despite all these regulations, by-laws and charter standards, ingested bacteria give us Scots more human fatalities per head of population than any other part of the EU.

In Amsterdam, however, we watched food-shop assistants licking surplus cream off their thumbs and fingers after they had used their bare hands to put four fancy pieces in front of us. We watched to see if they washed their hands afterwards, but they went straight back to serving the next customers.

We watched the staff in one Dutch lunch cafe whack out handfuls of boiled rice into takeaway containers. Yes, handfuls. With their bare hands.

We saw someone making up sandwiches in a cafe in the plush Magna Plaza centre while a dog end dangled from his mouth.

Most strikingly of all, we were sitting having an indoor fly cup beside the Tuschinsky Theatre, in a swish tearoom whose entire front was open to the street, when Mrs Harper, who was facing the street, tapped my feet with hers and nodded behind me. I turned round expecting to see yet another transvestite. Instead, I saw a couple of pigeons sauntering down the aisle between the tables.

I was half-thinking about drawing the staff's attention to their verminous guests when I realised that all three assistants behind the counter knew the doos were there, but weren't inclined to bother much.

Not even when one of the birds fluttered up on to the counter, then took a dive to perch on the lip of the tray of breads propped against the back wall did the staff so much as wave a lazy hand at them.

I took a look at my toasted teacake, which had come from that same tray only minutes before, and wondered what added ingredients I might have consumed courtesy of earlier winged visitors. But the clincher came when the second doo flapped up to sit on the glass counter, cocked its tail and relieved itself down the front of the display case.

Trust me; it's not easy to appreciate Dutch apple cake, no matter how well presented, when you're peering at it through a spattered curtain of doo do. No amount of cinnamon sprinkle retrieves the situation.

Only then did the staff see fit to move, and even that was pretty half-hearted. They carried on their conversation while one of them shambled towards the doos and waved them idly outside. Another went to get a damp cloth and wiped up the poop. I can't say that the cloth wasn't rinsed afterwards, but I had direct sight to the sink and I didn't see it get so much as a run under the tap.

Now, I'm not suggesting that the Netherlands is rife with mediaeval hygiene of a sort that would have kept Dickens writing for months. Equally, I can't say that it was a place obsessed by cleanliness in its food outlets. We saw the same sort of poor hygiene practice too often for that to be true.

So why is it that Scotland, regulated to a greasy spot, kills so many of its people, while Holland, where anything appears to be acceptable, is rated third-safest for food-related hygiene in the EU? It comes a shade behind Sweden and Denmark. I know. I've checked the figures.

Are the Dutch a naturally hardier breed? Are we 5million peer craiters just waiting for bugs to punch our lights out? Or is it a little bit of both?

It rather mocks many of our environmental-health regulations, if you ask me. My theory is that we're so obsessed with kitchen sprays, antiseptic cloots and anti-bacterial Fairy Liquid that when any self-respecting bug does come along we don't have the immunity to it that we should have and it knocks us for six.

Medical opinion could probably trounce me on a dozen different counts, but I can't think of any other explanation. We've become so obsessively clean that we're easy targets. The Dutch, who seem to follow the old Scots maxim: "Ye'll aet a wheen o dirt afore ye're deid", appear to sail past listeria, legionnaire's, salmonella and everything else without so much as a faint stomach rumble.

Far from tightening controls, maybe the time has come to slacken them a bit.

Far from banning children from farms in case they step in dubs, take a whole schoolful, line them up against the byre wall and spray them with the slurry pump.

It was a mildly distracted Mr and Mrs Harper who stepped out into Kalverstraat that afternoon, I can tell you. So distracted were we, that I almost missed the sight of our holidays. Crowds were parting before us and it was a few seconds before I saw why.

Coming towards us was a man in his late 20s, quite thin, about 6ft.2in. He wore a leather puffball hat, a woman's shoulder-length black wig and full make-up. Round his neck was a silver choke chain, below which he was encased in a leather corset with push-up bra.

Black fishnet stockings and patent-leather stilettos completed his ensemble. I was so taken aback that I stopped to watch, while trying not to watch, if you know what I mean, as he passed me and carried on. The back view was even more bizarre than the front. Corset and stockings apart, he was naked.

We don't get a lot of that in the howe. Well, apart from Hogmanay 1979.

It made me feel very unworldly to be so astonished, because nobody else appeared to be bothered.

In fact, to be very politically incorrect, it made me feel queasy.

Without any doo assistance, either.

Again, people wondered if I had embellished the punchline to this story. I certainly hadn't. You see some extremely strange things in Amsterdam, and this mannie was one of the strangest.

The most comical thing of the lot was the reaction of a group of Manchester lads who were obviously out for a stag weekend. They bowed impeccably and grinned as Leather Gear strutted past them.

They said nothing, but I can lip-read enough to recognise a round of silent expletives when I see it.

4. THE WORLD HAS GONE MAD

Or why to worry less about criminals and more about victims

━━ ━━ ━━ ━━

"Either the world has taken leave of its senses or I'm
missing something fundamental in each of several
of the top news stories of the past week."

IT HAS been an imperspicuous week in the howe. I'm sorry that we're going to have to be serious today, because something bizarre must have happened while I was on holiday. Either the world has taken leave of its senses, or I'm missing something fundamental in each of several of the top stories of the past week.

To begin with the most trivial, BT and telecoms watchdog Oftel have been issuing notices every week for the past 18 months warning that dialling codes would change in six key areas of the UK. They encouraged people to begin using the new codes early to get used to them before the old codes went defunct.

They pleaded with the media to help spread the word. They warned businesses to reset their switchboards. They badgered domestic users to reprogram speed-dial phones. The tone became increasingly heavy as the day approached.

What happened? The country emerged relatively unscathed, except for BT, which forgot to reprogram its 1471 system.

In Edinburgh and Fife, the two councils want a hefty increase in Forth Road Bridge tolls. Why? To discourage drivers from using the bridge. This is an interesting business model that deserves study by other industrial sectors.

Airlines could double fares to stop seats wearing out so quickly and save on in-flight catering costs. Magazines could treble their cover price to save on ink. Hotels could quadruple their room rate and save a fortune on laundry. A gold-seal strategy.

In Amsterdam, a guide is being published for tourists, explaining where and how to get high on drugs without making nuisances of themselves. There is also a section on how to hire a suitable prostitute and emerge unscathed. The guide isn't the work of some seditious underground publishing house; it's by the Amsterdam Police.

As far as we know, there is no truth in the rumour that the sequel will be a police manual on how to burgle while causing minimal damage, and how to batter someone senseless without bruising your knuckles.

The madness gets a little more extravagant now. We all know that Zimbabwe is on the brink of anarchy. Some would say that it has toppled already and that even Mugabe has lost control of his war veterans. This ragbag of supposed soldiers, according to one military strategist, shows signs of contemporary military discipline, but that's another tale.

On the day that a second white farmer was shot dead, the Foreign Office sent a telegram to Mugabe congratulating him on 20 years of independence. On the day that three black activists screamed at a BBC reporter that all whites were racist vermin (ponder that one) to be hunted down and exterminated, Robin Cook announced that the UK would give the murderers what they wanted and would fund land reform in Zimbabwe.

Yet Britain has no responsibility to fund land reform. All duties were discharged formally and legally on Independence Day in 1980. Britain set a dangerous precedent when it spent £44million buying white-owned land in 1986 for the Harare Government to redistribute to poor black share-croppers. You won't be surprised to learn that every last acre of that land went to Mugabe's cronies in Harare.

What does Mr Cook imagine has changed this time round, apart from the fact that Mugabe is more unhinged, more desperate to cling to power and that this new Whitehall policy teaches the world that Britain will kneel to anyone who grabs headlines with sufficient violence?

The Opposition in Zimbabwe is horrified by Mr Cook's offer. A friend of mine, Mark Chavunduka, a journalist in Harare, says that the Foreign Office has misread the situation entirely and is flinging petrol at the flames. He despairs for millions of ordinary blacks who are as fearful for their families as white farmers are for theirs.

Neither can he see the sense of an African leader looking for a scapegoat for the economic ills that 20 years of his own misrule have created, then plumping for the sector which brings in 40% of the national income. That takes a special kind of madman.

Not quite as mad, just substantially raivelled, is the nonsense in Miami over Elian, the Cuban boy whom America has decided should be sent back to Cuba, as requested by his Cuban father. This decision has angered Florida Cubans, but does anyone really care about this apart from a few thousand heid cases who seem a wee bit more excitable than is healthy?

Unless I've missed something, the boy was stuck in a house for five months with relatives he had barely met, who were asked repeatedly to allow him to a chaperoned meeting with his father, but who stalled, then lied and eventually retreated into hermitage completely.

When agents found him, he was spending time in a wardrobe with a Pentecostal preacher and an alcoholic fisherman while, streaked on the floor outside, his "uncle" was too blootered to know what was happening. A loving home, indeed.

His female cousin, a quaintly haggard 21-year-old who seems to have been through the mill a few times, says she is distraught that Washington has abused a six-year-old boy.

What she means is that she is distraught that she and an unruly mob have lost the best photo opportunity they've had in the 41 years since Castro rose to power. The Feds might have used a heavy hand, but the end has (almost) justified the means.

If the world deplores abuse of Elian, it should ponder the motives of a family which pretends it is looking after a six-year-old when it's really coveting a pawn in a bigger political game.

Finally, we come to the Norfolk farmer who was jailed for

murder 16-year-old burglar Fred Barras or, as we all know now, ex-burglar Fred Barras. We should have seen this coming perhaps, but a victim-support charity is making noises about getting involved to fight for justice. It feels that compensation might be due — to Burglar Fred's family.

You can hear it now. "Deprived childhood . . . blah-blah . . . absent father . . . blah-blah-blah . . . never had a chance . . . blah-de-blah-de-blah . . ."

Multitudes of Britons, young and old, had and have deprived childhoods, absent fathers and few opportunities, but are still sufficiently decent not to lay waste to their neighbourhoods and abuse innocents in the way the Barras brood did. It would instructive to see if the bleeding hearts would still bleed were their grandmothers to be mugged, their wives assaulted, their daughters raped and their homes burgled. The Barras dispatch was unfortunate, but better to think of the real victims for a change.

Now that the compensation notion has been broached, you may be sure that the usual gaggle of rumbly-jumblies and social apologists won't be far behind with their hand-wringing and demands for formal apologies. What to say to such people?

Take a couple of Prozac, pop yourself into bed and you might be feeling a wee bit brighter in the morning.

■■■ ■■■ ■■■ ■■■

This one drew a heated response. One reader wanted me sacked and another left a series of abusive and anonymous messages on my voicemail. Furious as he was, he wasn't bright enough to realise that voicemail logs all calls, and that we would get BT to trace them. BT located him instantly and put him, his address and his phone number on its perverts register. No messing.

5. TINSELTOWN'S RULES

Or why movie convention doesn't stand close scrutiny

■■ ■■ ■■ ■■

*"It set me to thinking about the various rules of movie
shorthand that speed a story along, but ruin it at the same
time because of a complete lack of sense or logic."*

IT HAS been a sophistic week in the howe. It must have been
a slack Friday evening, for I was chatting to the Press and
Journal's film critic, Tom Forsyth, about the various movies he
had seen recently. The two latest were Galaxy Quest, some sort of
Star Trek spoof, and Scream 3, another sequel in the teen-horror
series for the hard of rational thought.

He mentioned that the most memorable character in Galaxy
Quest was not one of the leads, but one of the supporting roles,
known only as Crewman Six. If you're familiar with the old Star
Trek TV series from the late 1960s, you'll get the joke at once.

In almost every Star Trek episode, there was one crewman who
had never appeared before. Since the lead actors were on long-
term contract and couldn't be bumped off, whenever the script
called for a grisly death at the hands of some extra-terrestrial
being, a Crewman Six would be brought on for the express
purpose, 15 minutes later, of expiring.

It became one of the unwritten rules of Star Trek that as soon as
an unfamiliar face appeared in crewman's uniform, the audience
knew he would be dispatched 15 minutes later.

I told Tom that I had very little time for horror films, either, since
their plots were always full of holes. Why, for instance, when a

character in a haunted house is told: "Whatever you do, keep your door locked", is the first thing she does on hearing a noise to unlock the door, go outside and start exploring?

It set me to thinking about the various rules of movie shorthand that speed a story along, but ruin it at the same time because of a complete lack of sense or logic.

I confess I noticed this first when I was in my early teens and mad about cars. One of my favourite movies was Bullitt, the picture in which Steve McQueen gets involved in probably the most famous car chase in movie history, thundering and roaring up and down the hilly streets of San Francisco.

I don't even recall why I started counting his gearchanges, but on the fourth or fifth time I saw the film I watched the chase purely to tot up the number of times in succession that McQueen changed up. By my reckoning, that car had the only 13-speed manual gearbox in automotive history. Next time it comes on TV, you'll see what I mean.

Another unwritten rule of car chases, although mostly in low-budget TV series such as Starsky and Hutch, was that every chase had to involve driving into a pile of empty cardboard boxes. In James Bond movies, that becomes a market stall selling fruit.

Equally, when a speeding car heads for a crossroads, it sails through seconds before four cars arrive at the crossroads with split-second timing and collide.

When that same car is pursued along a freeway, all the other cars are always driving in obligingly staggered positions so that pursued and pursuer may weave in and out at will.

When an articulated lorry crosses the road ahead of the chase, the fleeing car is always sufficiently low to pass under the trailer, while the pursuer's car is always a couple of inches too tall and, thus, gets its roof ripped off.

If the fugitive has to get out of the car and flee on foot, he is always sufficiently dense to run up the middle of the street when anyone who was less of a neep would jink into a shop.

If he does see sense and run up an alley, mercy me, it's always a dead end, with a wall or chain-link fence just high enough to delay him so that his pursuer has time to race up, drag him back by the ankles and give him a good kicking. Horror films have the same shorthand. Why, for instance, when a character who is alone in an empty house hears a noise, does he bother calling: "Joe/Bob/Jeremy? Is that you?"? Because it never is.

Why, if there is a shot of a doorknob, does it start turning ve-e-e-e-ery slowly?

In war movies, why do characters show off photos of their sweetheart, since this apparently guarantees that they will be shot, blown up or dismembered within the next 10 minutes?

In thrillers, when a person climbs into an air-conditioning system to effect his escape, why is it always lit by more bulbs than there are in Piccadilly Circus? Why does his noisy clambering in all that plate steel always take him right over the very room where the baddies are discussing their heinous plans, yet they never hear him?

Why are all night-watchmen incompetent?

Why, when a man and a woman are running away from anything, will the woman always trip, fall and have to be helped from that point on?

Why does someone who has to escape from a building always run upstairs?

Why, when a character says: "Darling, I couldn't be happier" is her life a cataclysmic sotter within the next minute and a half?

Why, whenever a toilet appears in a film, is it never being used for the purpose for which it was intended? Why is it always used to hide, kill, get involved in hanky-panky or deal drugs?

Why is no bad guy black these days? Is every black person a paragon of virtue? The same goes for Italians.

Equally, why are English accents heard only from sinister baddies, butlers or homosexuals (or all three)?

Why do computer keyboards always beep and chatter? I've worked with them for more than 20 years and haven't come across any that do this. Why do warning messages appear on computer screens letter by letter and in type that is red and four inches high? I haven't come across that either.

How do you spot the car that will be wrecked by the end of the film? Look for the ones that are at least six or seven years old.

Guaranteed. Also, if you're watching a 1960s British thriller series, the white MkII Jaguar will always go over a cliff in the last five minutes.

Why, when a car is pushed over a cliff, does it explode in a mid-air ball of fire half a second before it hits the ground?

In The Italian Job, when the Mafia bulldozes more than £200,000 worth of exotic cars over the edge of an Italian alpine road, how did the cars get there in the first place? None of them has an engine.

Try holding your breath for as long as any movie character has to survive below water. Take a lungful the second the character goes under and see how well you last. No matter how fit and young you are, I guarantee that you won't even come close.

Not even against Shelley Winters in the Poseidon Adventure, who seems to last for four minutes and 17 seconds. Not bad for a big girl.

These are just 30 or so of Movieland's obvious rules that spring to mind. You'll no doubt have many more of your own.

Try looking out for these and others the next time you sit down in front of the TV or go to the cinema. It perks up the enjoyment factor no end.

━━ ━━ ━━ ━━

This column was one of three in this book that was nominated for a national award. I confess that I can't abide awards of any sort. They're known in the trade as pots and the people who go after them are pothunters. That's not a compliment. Just do your job and get on with it; that's my view.

Anyway, I didn't go to the ceremony at the posh London hotel, which is just as well as I didn't win.

6. FIVE YEARS OF CANINE COMPANY

Or why man's best friend can be a challenge

■■ ■■ ■■ ■■

*"I could do without the wet kisses after he has dined and
the occasional loud reports that flutter his haunches, sting
the back of your throat and peel the paint off the walls."*

IT HAS been a therianthropic week in the howe. My brother
asked me a curious question the other day. "Knowing what
you know now," he said, "would you still have got yourselves
the dog?"

The implication in the question was that, in some way, I had
regretted welcoming our new arrival in 1995.

I will admit that, on occasion, I have despaired silently that his
command of English doesn't stretch beyond responding to Sit,
Stay, Lie, Stop, Here, Heel, Water, Grub and Get Out of There
Right Now, for it would be interesting to know what was going on
behind those big brown eyes.

I could do without the wet kisses after he has dined and the
occasional loud reports that flutter his haunches, sting the back of
your throat and peel the paint off the kitchen walls, although I
admire his insistence that these have nothing to do with him, for
he looks round casually, as if curious to know what has just
happened.

It pains me that we can walk for miles together in the country
and thoughts of his bowels and bladder will not cross his mind,
but as soon as he hears a car engine he'll wait until just the right
moment before lifting his leg or sending the tail out like a red

hairy poker and squatting for the entertainment of all. He has a showman's instinct for his ablutions.

In his early years, I used to fix him with a stare if he had misbehaved, but he learned very quickly just to stare back. So then I used to lean a little closer to him, to see if that put him off. But all he would do was carry on staring and hold up a paw.

So then I would lean a little closer still and whisper: "Vet's scissors."

That worked fine until the day, hashed for time, I left the washing out in the rain and did something else that must have been heinous. I believed Mrs Harper would take my minor oversights in good part, since these are generally so few and far between, but she sat down beside me, leaned close and whispered: "Vet's scissors."

Like many dogs, he has an unsettling habit of studying his co-residents: us. I have little time for the anthropomorphic notions of people who tell me: "Oh, they know every word you say", when clearly these are just animal characteristics and reaction to your tone of voice, but his constant look can put you off your stot if he keeps it up for long enough.

It's especially unsettling when he holds his head in that haughty way that setters have; looking along his muzzle, eyes half-dipped, as if he disapproves of something, but is too polite to say. He reminds me a lot of George Sanders or Jean-Claude Pascal, that old French boulevardier.

Like the eyes in a Rembrandt portrait, his gaze follows me round the room. Mrs Harper tells me that it's because "he's devoted to the leader of the pack", but I have a suspicion that it's more: "How soon is that grumpy blighter going to clear off so I can snaffle a bit of chocolate sponge off the old lady?"

Because that's how it is with all dogs. The three rules for having an obedient four-legged companion are Belly, Belly and Belly. The things are ruled by their stomachs, and ours is no exception.

But the original question? Would we still have got him had we known about the many drawbacks of owning a dog?

Unquestionably yes, for although the drawbacks are many, and dogs certainly tie you down whatever devotees tell you, the benefits far outweigh the burdens — especially when he's at the back door to greet you and not just the tail is wagging, but the whole rear end is going furiously as if he's trying to break himself in two.

All of which brings me to a story I heard a wee while back. It's probably an old joke, but it tickled me. It seems that a widower worthy from the country was pottering away at home, as usual, when the doorbell rang.

There, on the doorstep, stood his old Army buddy, long since emigrated to Canada and now back on native soil, probably for the last time.

They stood and looked at each other momentarily, then broke into a fit of backslapping and roaring with laughter. Our worthy invited his old pal inside to partake of some good old Scottish hospitality.

After 20 minutes' chat covering all the broad bases, the host thought it might be a good idea to persuade his old pal to stay for something to eat and a drink. After all, Canada's a long way without a dram. The guest agreed eagerly.

So the host called through his faithful collie, Ben. He reached into his jaicket pooch and pulled out a £20 note. Then he leaned into the fireside press and pulled out an old wicker basket that had belonged to his late wife.

He rested the arm of the basket in the dog's mouth and tucked the £20 into the dog's collar.

"Right, Ben," he said. "Awa tae the butcher's for a half-pun o sassidges. Then roon by the grocery for twa pints o milk and a loaf. On the road back, nip in past the pub and get a half-bottle."

The old dog looked up for a moment, basket still in his mouth, then trotted through to the kitchen, out of the back door and was gone.

"You gotta be joking," said the Canadian visitor. "You talk to your dog and you really expect him to remember all those instructions?"

Our worthy tapped the side of his nose. "Jist you wait and see," he said. "Ben's nae ordinary dog." The Canadian shook his head and laughed.

They carried on newsing for 20 minutes and then, just as they were beginning to feel dry kind, the front doorbell rang.

Our host looked at the mantelpiece clock and scowled. He hauled himself out of his seat and went to the front door. Still in the living-room, the Canadian could hear a raised voice, then the sound of something getting a good skelping, followed by a dog's yelps and wails.

A few moments later, the host appeared with the wicker basket in his hand. He was dark of visage and furrowed of brow. Inside the basket were the half pound of sausages, two pints of milk, a loaf and the all-important half-bottle.

"I could have sworn I heard you smacking your dog," said the Canadian.

"Ye did that," said the host, clattering the stuff out on his kitchen table.

"Was that because he missed something from your list?"

"Not a thing. The hale lot's here."

"He got everything? Wow, that's some dog you got. So how could you bring yourself to abuse a smart dog like that?"

"Because that's the second time this month he's forgotten his door key."

━━ ━ ━ ━

It took Stronach a long time to grow out of being a puppy. Even now, he has relapses into daftness. However, he is one of the few dogs we know who can be trusted to be left on his own for an hour or two and not go exploring or do damage. He won't even eat unless he has company. I wish we could claim that we had trained him to do this, but he just seemed to learn of his own accord.

7. ALTERNATIVE THERAPY

Or why to worry when the pills and potions come out

■ ■ ■ ■

*"There is now a suspiciously large brown-glass jar in the
bathroom containing what look like 100 small lucky
tatties, but which smell like camel dung."*

I T HAS been a bobbish week in the howe. You find us in good
spirits thanks largely to a new dietary regime which Mrs
Harper has been following from one of the weirder Sunday
supplements. Her spirits are high because she finds it healthful
and stimulating. Mine are up because I just think it's wonderful
entertainment.

It has been worrying me for some months that she seems more
and more fascinated by alternative therapies, of the kind usually
espoused by the beard-and-sandals brigade.

I find her sniffing lavender essence in the evening to help her to
sleep. Starflower oil capsules are supposed to keep her shiny. Malt
extract helps brain function. You know the sort of thing.

She rubs peppermint lotion into her feet each evening before
bed. It's like sleeping in a pandrop factory. Every other night,
there's a cod-liver-oil capsule to help her joints. Pandrops and fish:
what a restful combination.

Then there are the tiny wee tablets of stuff called pulsatilla.
Heaven knows what they do, but she has begun mumbling Italian
in her sleep.

All this is fine by me. She's her own boss. But now a campaign
appears to be under way to rope me into this agglomeration of

39

peels and potions. She has been insisting that I eat plenty of bananas (high in potassium) and broccoli (helps prevent testicular and prostate cancer).

There is now a suspiciously large brown-glass jar in the bathroom containing what look like 100 small lucky tatties, but smell like camel dung. I am waiting for the softening-up process to begin whereby these become part of my breakfast between now and the end of the year.

I can tell you in confidence that she will be disappointed. Even if she informs me that these tablets are supposed to replace my current greying hair with my old lustrous black locks, she will find, a few weeks hence, that our dog has become the first black-haired red setter in Scotland.

I make only one concession to alternative medicine, and that's only because I have found that it actually works.

First, I should tell you that I haven't eaten red meat in almost 20 years. Before farmers' wives write to tell me what a traitor I am in these straitened times for the Scottish beef industry, I should stress that it's just a personal thing. I don't like the taste or the texture, any more than I like the taste of eggs, blue cheese, Sunny Delight or Ferrero Rocher chocolates. It's not a philosophy, just a mark of pernicketyness.

Then, about 10 years ago, I began to feel perpetually wabbit. I had to haul myself out of bed, shambled through the day and slept for most of what little time I had to myself. I put this down just to the demands of the workload at the time. But when it persisted through a couple of fortnights' holidays, it became clear that something had to be done.

A colleague suggested that it had a lot to do with my meat-free diet, and not my workload. Are you so tired that you can't be bothered with anything, she said? Can you not summon the energy to tackle even the smallest, trivial jobs about the house? Do you fly off the handle with the least provocation?

I was guilty on all three counts, which she diagnosed as the classic symptoms of a Vitamin B shortage. I'm sorry if this is beginning to sound like a pill-popper's tract, but bear with me.

She said she'd had a boss several years before who had gone

completely veggie. Everyone had noticed a rosier bloom about the cheeks, but after a couple of years they noticed he was also a good deal more irascible. Staff behinds were being kicked (metaphorically) for minor misdemeanours. He was flying into rages for no apparent reason.

Being his PA, she put him on a daily Vitamin B Complex tablet and, hey presto.

"What?" I said. "He stopped being coorse to his employees?"

"No," she said. "He was just as coorse to them, but at least he laughed and smiled while he did it."

(All right, I made up that last bit.)

She said the first problem with Vitamin B was that while committed vegetarians knew they should take it as a supplement, fussy eaters had no idea. The second problem was that sceptics who had been advised to try Vitamin B Complex tablets tended to take them for a couple of weeks, notice no difference and give up, whereas it generally took a couple of months for the effects to kick in.

And, loath though I am to admit this, she was right.

It worked.

I persisted with a little tub of 100 of the things that I bought from Boots. I persisted only because they cost £4, and I was blowed if I was going to give up and waste £2.50, even although they tasted like banana-flavoured chalk.

I've been taking them daily for 10 years and haven't looked back. On the few occasions I've gone abroad and forgotten to take a supply with me, I know all about it within three or four days. And, no, I don't believe it's psychological. And I certainly don't believe all that guff on the side of Kellogg's packets about one serving providing 30% of your daily vitamins. I used to eat three servings a day and still suffered.

So, for what it's worth, if you're not a great meat-eater and you're always tired, worrisome and irritable, you're probably suffering a shortage of Vitamin B. Of course, you could be just a genuine ratbag.

Which brings me to Mrs Harper's latest fad. I arrived in the kitchen on Sunday morning to find an array of packets of linseeds, sunflower seeds, pumpkin seeds, pine seeds, sesame seeds and seed seeds. There were jars of extract, cartons of soya milk, stem ginger, fancy flour and little stalky things that smelled like the bottom of a wardrobe.

"It's energy cake," she said. "It's not for you. It's for me. It's recommended."

"By seed growers, I suppose," I said.

"Seeds give you energy," she said. "It's natural food and wholesome."

"Remind me to close the windows and warn the neighbours," I said. "Maybe the Met Office, too."

She went ahead, anyway, and kirned up this mixture, which she then covered with clingwrap and left to sit for a couple of hours. I peered in once or twice. All I can say is that if a farmer saw that lying beside a heifer in the morning, he'd phone the vet.

She cooked it (Gas 5, 190C, 375F for 75 minutes) and out came something that looked like a wet brown brick. She has been chewing a slice every morning and a slice every evening for the last three days.

Have I noticed a difference? Indeed, I have.

Every time she passes the lobby mirror, she pecks it.

▬ ▬ ▬ ▬

The latest fad is a nasal spray for headaches. I inquired if this was meant to cure them or to induce them, but the humour wasn't appreciated.

The camel-dung lucky tatties came and went with no discernible difference in our health. I'm still on the Vitamin B Complex, which I commend to anyone who feels as if modern life is just a little too hectic for comfort.

8. NATION'S FAVOURITE GRANDMOTHER

Or why the Queen Mother enjoyed a century of respect

■ ■ ■ ■

*"The Queen Mother has mastered the art of being
appealing to all and offensive to none. This is a skill
which every politician covets."*

THE story goes that a spat had broken out. The notoriously
gay below-stairs ensemble of Clarence House had been
split into three camps by a disagreement. Some retainers
were flouncing around in the huff. Some were desperate to
scratch out an eye or two. Some were just sulking or stamping
their little feet.

The tantrums were bad enough, but they had thrown into chaos
the normally ordered progression of life upstairs. The Queen
Mother stood it until she felt obliged to call a footman to inquire
why her evening meal was already 20 minutes late. The footman
explained that there had been a bit of contretemps among some
of the more colourful staff.

The Queen Mother retorted: "My compliments to the old queens
down there, but this old queen is hungry and she wants her
dinner."

The tale might well be apocryphal because insights into the
Queen Mother's humour, opinions and politics are scarce. Analyse
any biography of the last 50 years in which she has appeared and
note how few documented public statements can be attributed to
her. Notice how few flashes of wit or acerbic asides can be corroborated. This is not accidental.

The Queen Mother has mastered the art of being appealing to all and offensive to none. She is the ultimate practitioner of a skill which every politician covets. She is the pre-eminent spindoctor, with a public image and capacity to inspire affection which cross generations and are peerless.

She does it by saying nothing on record, but working tirelessly out of the public eye. Brilliant.

This is not to say that Her Majesty is bland. Friends and staff have spoken in unguarded moments of a woman with probably the sharpest sense of humour in the Monarchy. They tell of a woman of immense compassion for, and interest in, even the humblest member of her household.

They tell also of a woman who is in no doubt about her national standing, and that of all the Royal Family, she is certainly the most demandingly royal; having been raised in an era when the Monarchy's place in the fabric of British life was not quite as assailable as it is now.

The extraordinary thing is that virtually none of her staff grudges her these privileges or her extraordinarily demanding regime. They genuinely like her because she seems genuinely to like them.

Journalists who have covered Royal events post-war have all noticed an extraordinarily simple trick which the Queen Mother uses to work her PR magic. Most other members of the family walk slowly past the assembled crowds, stopping here and there to receive flowers and smiling generally at the crowd as a single entity.

The Queen Mother alone has made an art of stopping to look directly at individual people with those piercing china-blue eyes, and smile, perhaps chat, before moving on. All who have experienced it have remarked on how personally interested she seemed to be, not realising that they are the latest to have been seduced by one very polished public performer. She's had 100 years to practice, after all.

Even a casual glance through the records shows the Queen Mother's zest for life. Some of her asides would grace any comedy script. Once, she was assailed on a tour of Africa by an extremely irate African who resented British colonial power. Instead of having the man bundled off and punished, she stayed the security people and listened patiently.

Once he had run out of steam, and his ranting at the English rape of his country and his people had petered to a low peep, she placed a consoling hand on his forearm, smiled and said: "I know how you feel. I'm Scottish myself." Journalists say she walked on, leaving him smiling and swooning. Another one had fallen under the spell.

This extraordinary capacity for putting people at their ease is illustrated best by a story from another trip to Africa; this time a State tour of South Africa in 1947. The Royal Family had been given use of a luxury train for the 10-week tour and had tried to cover every type of community, from the bustle of Johannesburg and Cape Town, to the simpler pleasures of life in the villages.

At one stage, the train had stopped in a small veldt village of not more than 100 people and, since the party was running a little ahead of schedule, decided to overstay, which delighted the village.

This gave the Queen (as she was then) even more time to work her charm, and the shy and diffident King George VI was happy to let her make most of the effort, since that was her forte.

As the train began steaming up to depart, one delighted Afrikaaner farmer's wife managed to get the Queen to stop. "Now listen," the woman said. "It's been a delight to see you, dear. You and your hubby's welcome back here any time." And the Queen nodded graciously and thanked her kindly for the offer.

The Queen Mother also has a capacity for telling stories against herself. On a tour of Canada shortly before the death of the King, they appeared in a small Saskatchewan market town to be met with as much ceremony as the town could muster.

They were introduced to the mayor, who welcomed them graciously. During the visit, the King plucked up the courage to ask the mayor if he was, indeed, the man in charge of the town.

"I am, sir," the mayor said.

"I see," the King said. "It's just that I thought the mayor would have had a mayoral chain or some such badge of office."

"I do, sir."

"Really? You aren't wearing it for some reason, then."

"Well, sir, we keep it for special occasions."

The Queen Mother found, and still finds, the exchange highly amusing. She also has an endearing capacity to be self-deprecating. Once, she returned from an official engagement and announced to the household that she had invited a couple of American millionaires to lunch.

"And we must remember to put in an effort to impress them," she advised. "These people are quite wealthy."

But perhaps my favourite story illustrates quite how easy can be the relationship between Her Majesty and some of her older, more trusted retainers. The story goes that one of the Clarence House gardeners had gone on holiday to Russia, which was quite a novel concept in the political austerity of the early 1970s.

So intrigued was the Queen Mother that she asked if she might have a word with the man on his return. He was pottering in the potting shed on his first day back when his boss showed up.

"Russia?" she said.

"Yes, ma'am."

"But why Russia, of all places?"

"Well, ma'am, there's some really lovely places, and some really beautiful palaces in Leningrad. And, if I may be so bold, ma'am, the Hermitage makes Buck'n'ham Pellis look like a prefab."

The QM is said to have been smiling to herself as she left.

——— ——— ——— ———

You'd be suprised by how many of even the most cynical journalists were charmed by the wit and grace — and steel — of the Queen Mother, one of the greatest figures of the UK's 20th century.

9. CUSTOMER COMPLAINTS

Or why there are as many chancers in front of the counter

▬ ▬ ▬ ▬

*"Very few of us would have jobs without customers,
but the customer is king? Pull the other one. It's fine
in theory, but it's divorced woefully from reality."*

IT HAS been a furacious week in the howe. You might have
spotted in the Press and Journal a few days ago that one
major retail chain in the UK reckoned it was losing around
£48million a year to theft.

That wasn't strictly accurate. The company wasn't actually losing
£48million a year. It was merely loading £48million on to the
prices paid by the rest of us, which is not quite the same thing.

This is partly why I have never held much with the buzz phrase
of modern British business: the customer is king. You hear
everyone from the Trade Secretary to the chief executive of the
fledgling e-commerce concern declaiming that the customer is
king, and lecturing staff to accommodate the client wherever
possible.

It would be foolish to pretend that customers aren't important to
business. Very few of us would have jobs without them. But the
customer is king? Pull the other one. It's fine in theory, but it's
divorced woefully from reality. Too many modern British
customers are a combination of arm-chancer, wide boy, liar, spiv
and egotist all rolled up in one distasteful package. Ask anyone
who has to deal with them on the front line.

Ask the people at Marks and Spencer who have what is

probably the least savoury job in the whole of British commerce. They're the sniffers. They're the people who take back exchanged clothes and have to sniff the oxters and crotches to try to establish if clothes have been worn and, thus, not eligible for refund.

Can you imagine a more depressing nine to five? Can you imagine anyone looking forward less to the hot days of summer? Can you imagine the career path? "Miss Robertson, good news. You've done so well on T shirts that we're promoting you to swimming trunks. If you do well there — keep your nose to the grindstone, as it were — in six months you could be on the all-in-ones."

I met a Markies departmental manager a couple of Christmases ago at one of those tedious dos when you stand around with a salmon vol-au-vent, being bored stiff by complete strangers telling you what's wrong with your industry and where, out of deference to your hostess, you can't grab the bore's tie and say: "Pardon me, but you're a complete ignoramus. Kindly step to the left before I hang this vol-au-vent off the end of your nose."

Anyway, this very pleasant Markies woman told me that the customer-service department in any M&S store was judged to be the most harrowing posting for a member of staff. It was the equivalent of the gulags. She suspected that some managers used it as a punishment posting.

She said that customers sometimes tried to pass off as new, five-year-old garments which had been worn maybe once or twice. These customers were sufficiently fly to hang on to the labels in order to reattach them, albeit crudely.

Alas, they were unaware that each label carried a code for date of manufacture. When this was run through the computer and showed that the pair of breeks or summer top or winter coat had been stocked from February to June in 1994, a few were graciously embarrassed at being collared, most affected ignorance, but an increasing number became belligerent and began reeling off what they thought were their rights.

Strictly speaking, their only rights were to take back the garment and beetle off, but a store has a major PR problem with such people. Does it bend the rules and lay itself open to repeat abuse, or does it stand its ground, risk losing business and suffer by the inevitable word of mouth?

The customer is king? Ho-ho.

One of my colleagues told me that he once went to dinner at one of Aberdeen's most interesting restaurants with an oil-industry executive who prided himself on getting value for his expense-account money.

The oilman thought it was a marvellous wheeze, once the main course had been delivered, to sprinkle a few grains of sand or small stones somewhere among the vegetables or in the sauce, then call back the waiter and complain.

The ease with which the oilman did this suggested it was a skill born of long practice, and my colleague was horrified: not just that the man was inordinately proud of what was basically dishonesty, but that, by extension, he was being incriminated himself by being in on the scam. Half the time, the oilman said, self-satisfaction dripping from him, a restaurant manager would authorise 50% off the bill or offer a free bottle of wine.

It wasn't that the oilman's firm couldn't stand the cost of a table d'hote meal; it simply stoked the host's ego to know that he had put one over on another firm. You're right: a very sad case.

My favourite, however, if favourite is the word, concerns a tale that has passed into business legend in the Inverness area. The managing director of a major company had received a complaint from the owner of a small business nearby.

The detail of the complaint is lost in the mists now, but the letter had a bitter tone about being let down and perhaps reconsidering doing business in future. Naturally, the MD didn't want to lose any business, small or large, and summoned the appropriate staff to ask what had gone wrong.

The staff didn't believe that anything had gone wrong at all. If anything, the customer company had had sterling service throughout, almost to the point of excessively generous terms. They suggested that their MD call the other man's bluff.

At that, the MD flew into a rage and treated the hapless staff to a five-minute lecture. Were they cloth-eared? Didn't they know that the customer was king? Did they imagine that they would have jobs if they treated clients so disdainfully? He concluded by ordering them down to the customer to offer a sympathetic ear and to negotiate.

At a very uncomfortable meeting, the customer couldn't come up with any specific complaint, which persuaded the visitors that he was chancing his arm after all, as they had long suspected. Although he couldn't come up with any complaint more concrete than a few bits of administrative trivia, he demanded the writing off of a bill for £14,000.

The two men were aghast at such boldness and said they would have to refer to their MD.

Their MD gulped but, in a showmanlike gesture, ripped up the £14,000 invoice in front of his staff and told them to go back with the good news. The customer was king. He prided himself on being a listening man. His firm's reputation would not be tarnished by incompetent minions for staff.

The chancer accepted the kind offer (there's a surprise) and that was supposedly the end of it.

Three weeks later, the chancer's firm went into receivership, but not before he took out all his money and hotfooted it to his yacht and villa in Portugal, where he has been ever since.

Not a word was said by the MD, who must have borne his embarrassment privately.

The customer, after all, was king.

▬ ▬ ▬ ▬

Anonymous letters addressed to me never get as far as my desk. They're binned by the people who open my mail. This column, however, brought a letter of thanks signed by "four weary and depressed shop assistants in Aberdeen".

Happy to help.

10. GIFTED WHEN IT COMES TO PRESENTS

Or why Christmas and weddings can be minefields

■ ■ ■ ■

"I think the couple should wait to be asked what they
would like instead of ramming their graspers under your
nose while the engagement ring's still warming up."

IT HAS been a tributary week in the howe. The kitchen table is strewn with catalogues from Ikea, catalogues from Muji and catalogues from all manner of supposedly up-market stores that no one outside Central London knew existed.

We are trying to find a wedding present.

I am at something of a disadvantage in this quest in that I have never met the couple-to-be. Even Mrs Harper has met only one half of it, a former colleague who has been keeping in touch on a Christmas-card basis for the last 10 years.

I'm not sure that this degree of friendship qualifies her for a wedding present, particularly as it's her second time out of the starting blocks and she would have had a present first time round, but I wouldn't dream of saying so to Mrs Harper.

I made the mistake on Monday evening, you see, of watching my beloved wade through some glossy catalogue of over-priced trinketry and musing: "Those 10 Christmas cards have been a good investment."

I was shot one of her familiar scowls across the top of the catalogue. "What do you mean?"

"She invests in your friendship by buying a Christmas card a year for 10 years — at best estimate about a tenner's worth every decade, postage and packing included — and you're about to treat her to a musical carriage-clock barometer with bottle-opener, alarm and built-in cigar lighter. I call that a healthy return. Does she have any stock market tips, I wonder."

Here's a wee bit of advice, readers. No matter how irked you might be, on no account query a woman's impending investment in a long-lost chum. To do so is to "reduce the bond of friendship to the grubbiness of a financial transaction".

In other words, I am perfectly right.

While I'm feeling curmudgeonly, I might as well rail at another wedding-ritual abomination: the list. I know that a circulated list of potential gifts eliminates all manner of problems for the happy couple, in that there is no prospect of their receiving six toasters, 14 bales of towels, three anglepoise lamps and no bedsheets.

I must be old enough, however, to have that uneasy feeling that it's touting for gifts. I know that's irrational in the current social climate, because a wedding gift is virtually guaranteed the minute you hear that the groom has got down on bended knee, but I happen to think that the couple should wait to be asked what they would like instead of ramming their outstretched graspers under your nose while the engagement ring's still warming up.

Besides, by the time these lists get to us all that's usually left are the £250 Swarovski Crystal table lamp, the £500 Thomas Cook honeymoon voucher and the £900 15.2cu.ft American-style fridge-freezer with fast freeze, self-defrost and ice dispenser.

Mrs Harper always looks half blankly and half in panic at these lists, then she looks at me as if I have the answer to her quandary. I always do. "Give them a bottle of Markies bath salts and be done with it," I tell her. "They can always take it back and change it for a dozen bananas."

Does she listen? No, she doesn't. Any more wedding lists and she'll have us bankrupt.

Which reminds me of a tale which became the speak of the place in the mid-1970s, when wedding lists were unheard of. A very avant-garde couple evidently had heard about the principle of wedding lists either in the States or in London, where both had been working prior to uniting in unholy matrimony.

This list caused bemusement in the various corners of the North and North-east where their respective relatives and acquaintances lurked, but everyone assumed that this was modern pre-wedding convention and that they had better swallow their irk and get on with it. One couple in our ken, a farmer near to retirement and his brosey (and hugely lovable) wife, thought that a new-fangled food-mixer would be nice, and studied the list to see if it was still unclaimed and, if so, what type was required.

No mixer had been signed up at that point, but they were aghast to discover that the required model was a top-flight Kenwood Chef costing the best past of £150. You have to understand that £150 was £150 in the mid-1970s, and these were people who knew the right side of a ha'penny. She'd been thinking of a battery-powered Chefette and he'd been thinking of a Tilley lamp with a spare wick.

They took themselves into Aberdeen one Saturday to see where would have the best price. They couldn't get it below £145. They repaired to a Mitchell and Muil and were horsing into half a fruit square each while deciding what to do.

Presently, our man relented. "I'll awa and get them their food mixer," he said. "There's nae eese you walkin aa the wye back tae the shop. I'll see ye at the car in an oor."

She turned up at the car on the dot to find him seated therein. "Did ye get their food mixer?"

He nodded at the back seat and she turned to see a wooden spoon with a ribbon tied round the neck.

He drove all the way home, his wife sweating and stewing, before he revealed that the £145 Kenwood Chef was in the boot.

My parents once gave the daughter of one of their acquaintances a tea service as a wedding gift. They had seen not hide nor hair of the daughter for nearly 10 years, because she had been off to university and then had been working non-stop in some Godforsaken hole or other. England, I think it was. Still less had they met the beau.

But that's the way we do things in the country. Older people don't give wedding presents as a means of helping a young marriage to a happy start. They give presents, even to people they have hardly seen, as a mark of the friendship that exists between themselves and the bride/groom's parents.

It wasn't a cheap tea service, either. It was one of those bone-china jobs with a crest stamped on the bottom of everything and with a flourish at the top of the handle on every cup, which I remember joking was a crannie-rest so they could be real fantoosh on a Sunday. And that was that.

A week after the honeymoon had been concluded, a letter arrived at my parents' house. It was the ritual thank-you note.

To their credit, it wasn't one of those pre-printed jobs with spaces for the couple to scribble in the blanks.

Albert and Daphne
would like to thank you for the

42-piece tea set
on the occasion of their wedding.
It was very much appreciated.

Instead, they'd had the decency to compose a proper thank-you letter. It gave details of their honeymoon (not all the details, you understand), but then came the thank-you bit, and it ran something like:

"So now we're just trying to get the house in order and we really must thank you for the tea set. It's in use all the time and you couldn't have picked a better gift. You got us out of a right pickle. We'd have been stuck with using the good set."

━━ ━━ ━━ ━━

Funnily enough, we got invited to noticeably fewer weddings after this column appeared. I maintain it was just coincidence and I'm not losing sleep about it, but Mrs Harper says she is not so sure.

11. PEERING UP THE FAMILY TREE

Or why genealogy can be fraught with danger

━━ ━━ ━━ ━━

*"The man had a tie at a jaunty angle, his Sunday-best
suit with a hankie fluttering from the breast pocket and
the most magnificent handlebar moustache you'll see."*

I T HAS been a phyletic week in the howe. I was handed an
envelope shortly before last weekend; one of those big
manilla jobs the size of a coffee-table book. It contained two
sheets of paper. One was a coloured photocopy of an old black-
and-white photograph. The other was a carefully typed chart of
names and dates.

The photograph showed 17 faces in individual oval frames.
They seemed to have been taken, and the picture laid out,
probably just before World War I, judging by the clothes, the hair
and the grain of the images.

In the centre were a man and a woman in their mid-40s. The
woman had her dark hair parted in the centre and drawn tight.
She wore a black crinoline, lightened only by a pendant and a
narrow lace collar.

The man had a tie at a jaunty angle, his Sunday-best suit with a
hankie fluttering from the breast pocket and the most magnificent
handlebar moustache you'll see.

They were surrounded on the edges by 15 younger people,
ranging in ages from about four to 24, two of them in military
uniform.

Clearly, it was a large family, and almost all the offspring resembled their mother, which was just as well, because the four-year-old who suits a handlebar moustache has yet to be invented.

I looked at my mother, for it was she who had handed me the picture. I was obviously meant to comment in some way, but since I had seen none of the pictures before and still less recognised anyone, I couldn't oblige.

"That's your great-grandmother and great-grandfather," she said.

I might have guessed, but you may take it that it was a surprise, even a shock, to be confronted by so many ancestors for the first time and all at once.

I took the picture to the light of the kitchen window for closer study.

It took me not a second to locate my late grandfather, aged nine or 10 by the look of him, also done up in his Sunday suit with collar and tie. With a little work, I could even place the three youngest of his siblings, having met them in my boyhood, and again at my grandfather's funeral in 1983.

One moved to Macduff as a young man and lived out his life there; one did the same at Brechin, and there was one whose eventual location escaped me.

The others, I'm afraid, were strangers. I had heard their names over the past four decades, but had never met them and still less knew what they looked like.

It is an extraordinary feeling to see an entire family like that and know that it is yours; that a quarter of yourself came from them; that without those people you would not exist.

Even now, almost a week on, I find myself returning to the picture to study it; to look at the expressions on those young faces, frozen in time almost a century ago, and to wonder.

The last of them, Molly, the pretty lassie with her long black hair and the velvet-and-lace Sunday pinafore, died at the age of 91 in a Banchory nursing home shortly before Christmas last year. With her passing, another chapter closed.

My great-grandmother has a pained expression in the picture; that stoic look you see in most photographs of turn-of-the-century matrons, as if she has weathered a lot, knows that she coped, but wonders how on earth she managed it.

She had 15 children, mark you, which would tire anyone. She bore her family over 22 years, from four days before her 20th birthday to six months after her 42nd. It's a wonder she had any time for her housework. She died, aged 70, in 1939.

My admirably fertile great-grandfather is glaring at the camera, as if enduring an ordeal in which he sees no value whatsoever. How wrong he was. Without that Sunday ordeal a century ago, his great-grandson would have been denied an introduction.

I was handed in that envelope only two sheets of paper, but it represented an immense amount of work. Not everyone is as lucky as I.

The son of one of those children, now living in East Anglia, had become intrigued by the family tree and had been assembling this and many other branches over the last decade. Until you try assembling your lineage from scratch, you have no idea how difficult it is, and I'm indebted to him.

He and thousands of others have been bitten by the genealogy bug; by the drive to find roots and a compulsion not to forget. I know this by the number of letters we get at the Press and Journal from within Scotland and from throughout the Commonwealth and the US, all from fourth- and fifth-generation descendants of North and North-east settlers, and all hoping that some of you can put another piece of the jigsaw in place for them.

Some are woefully inadequate. You would scarcely believe the number of letters we get asking, in barely more than a sentence: "Does anyone know Jimmy MacKenzie?" These come usually from across the Atlantic, where they seem to have a shaky grasp of how big Scotland is and how many Jimmy MacKenzies there are.

Others show a triumph of hope over expectation. These usually take the form: "Does anyone remember the Buchan family of Longside? Albert and Martha married in 1828 and had seven children. All information gratefully acknowledged."

It would be tempting to wonder how long these correspondents think we live in Scotland, but you must always remind yourself that these people are desperate to explore any avenue, hoping that something might turn up, however unlikely it might be.

Then there are the ones who include so much detail that you

wonder why they need anything more. "I'm trying desperately to find Elsie Boyd and her sister, Ina, late of 27 Bideaway Close, Anytown. Their father was the town butcher before he took up with the minister's wife in 1946 and disgraced the family. Elsie and Ina ran off to join the circus. Elsie met and married an American millionaire in 1952 and moved to 31 Caledonia Crescent, San Diego, where she was last heard of running a wholesale cosmetics business and poodle parlour. Ina stayed with the circus and would still be there had it not been for the unfortunate incident with the elephant."

Whatever, we try to help them all. Or, at least, we hope that you can.

Which brings me to my favourite tale of ancestors. In the days when I used to do talks, I appeared at Turriff Academy, where I explained that the Press and Journal could trace its history to 1748 and its founder, James Chalmers. Giggling started at the back of the class. Two of the boys pointed at a third and said: "His name's Chalmers."

"Well," I said. "Maybe our James Chalmers was one of your ancestors."

"No," said the boy.

"How do you know?"

"Hinna got ony ancestors."

━━ ━━ ━━ ━━

> *After this column appeared I had many letters*
> *from people asking for help in tracing relatives.*
> *The Press and Journal staff did the best they could*
> *with each, and I'm pleased to say that in at least*
> *one case the newspaper was able to pull together a*
> *long-separated brother and sister — one living in*
> *Perthshire, the other in Canada.*

12. ORDEAL IN A VILLAGE SHOP

Or why even the simplest child abuse can be traumatic

■ ■ ■ ■

*"I was only seven or eight. I had no idea what I was doing
to earn her loathing, so I couldn't correct it. I was in
a classic lose-lose situation."*

IT HAS been a vilipendious week in the howe. Some of you
will have read of the Manchester baker's shop assistant who
was convicted this week of assaulting a customer. The
customer's crime? She had ventured to suggest that so much
jewellery on a man handling food perhaps wasn't best hygiene
practice.

There are ways and ways of making a point, and we cannot
know if the woman in question had spoken gently or dripping
with sarcasm or somewhere in between. Customers can be all
sorts.

However sarcastically she might have spoken, there seems little
call for the assistant to have leaped the counter, grabbed her by
the coat and pinned her against the wall.

He was jailed for three months for common assault, and I can't
say that I'm surprised. Even hunting to be our most charitable, the
best we can say in his defence is that some people have a very
short fuse and perhaps the customer's hygiene observation was
the last straw in a day that had been filled with simmering
calamity.

Maybe his doughrings had gone oval. Maybe his fondant fancies
weren't fancy enough. Maybe his apple tarts had gone pear-

shaped. Maybe 101 things. Whatever, he'll be cooling off in Strangeways as you read this.

I've written before from the opposite perspective in the customer-assistant relationship; observing that many members of the public are little more than rank chancers, treating shop assistants with less courtesy than they would their dogs. I still believe it, and cringe whenever I see a puffed-up customer in action.

But I've known it from the other side of the fence, too, albeit a very long time ago when I was less able to defend myself. A shop assistant in the village took an extreme dislike to me.

That would be easy to believe were it happening today, I know, but back then I was only seven or eight and innocent of all offence.

When I say an extreme dislike, I mean violent. What made it all the more traumatic was that I had no idea what I was doing to earn her loathing, so I couldn't correct it. I was in a classic lose-lose situation.

From more than 30 years' remove, I can see that I was guilty of nothing at all; that she was just an ill-natured besom, venting all her own unseen frustrations and anger on someone small who couldn't (and wouldn't) answer back, but I had no way of knowing that at the time and suffered desperately and in silence.

She worked in a shop which exists no longer because the owner died and there was no one to take it on. At the time, she looked very grown-up and fierce, although I guess she was probably little more than 17, and certainly hadn't reached 20. I learned long before most seven-year-old boys that late teens were a difficult time for the female temperament.

It began in quite a small way. Most shop assistants in the village were (and are) cheery souls who would pass the time of day with their customers whether they were seven or 77. This one habitually said nothing.

I would ask for whatever my mother had sent me for, hand over the cash, take the change and the goods, and the whole transaction would be conducted in silence. The contrast to usual village practice seemed odd to me.

Then, one day, just as I was reaching up to the door handle to leave, I heard her mutter two words. They're not for repeating here, but the second one was "off".

Since there was no one else in the shop, I turned to look. She leaned across the counter, glared at me and repeated herself, very deliberately and with a heavy pause in the middle.

You'll think me very naive and of a very sheltered upbringing, but at seven I hadn't a clue what the phrase meant. The message was entirely clear, however, from her tone and her glare. I didn't wait for a second bidding.

From there, it spiralled downwards into a seven-year-old's nightmare. Presumably having enjoyed my shock at her first attempt, she began laying it on ever more thickly.

She would stand at the door so I couldn't get out. She would threaten to lock me in all night. She would knock things off the counter, then tell me it had been my fault and that her boss would be billing my parents for my stupidity. She would fling my change at me so that I had to run all over the floor picking it up.

The only time I was safe was when another customer was in the shop. I used to stand there in the queue, feeling very small and forlorn, praying that someone would come in behind me and save me from another five minutes of abuse.

I used to dread walking to school, for she would be standing behind the counter, arms folded, watching me pass. Even more, I used to dread being sent for something from that shop. I remember my stomach tightening every time my mother asked me to run an errand there.

Eventually, I used to walk off in the direction of the shop, take a detour once I was out of sight of the house, wait for a couple of minutes, then walk home and say that the shop had run out of whatever it was I had been sent for.

This would have worked towards the end of a day but, on reflection, my mother must have been suspicious whenever the shop had run out of its staple produce at 8.30 on a Saturday morning.

Yet my mother had no reason to suppose that anything was wrong, for I couldn't bring myself to speak about it. I was almost as fearful of the consequences of clyping as I was of the regular ordeals in visiting the shop. Indeed, this is the first time I have spoken of it, and it's all down to the spark of a shop assistant's court case in Manchester.

So while my abuse was pretty mild stuff compared to the far greater traumas visited on too many children these days, it was desperate for me at the time. I can well understand why genuine child-abusers get away with their evil, and why their victims are equally determined not to confess, even although making a clean breast would fix it instantly — and certainly would have in my case.

All in all, I suppose my episode lasted for not more than six months, although it seemed a great deal longer at the time.

Maybe her half-year behind the counter was just a temporary job while she found something more befitting her talents (SS camp deputy torturer). Maybe her family moved away. Maybe she was sacked.

I don't know about any of that and, since I haven't seen the lady in more than 30 years and can't say I much cared for her at the time, I have no wish to know.

I suppose she must be a grandmother by now.

Heaven help her grandchildren.

I had a letter from a Moray man who said he had found this column genuinely distressing because he had endured much the same sort of irrational treatment and that he felt it had coloured the whole of his life and the way he related to others.

I wouldn't go as far as that in my case. It wasn't very pleasant at the time, but you just have to accept that some people are wired up strangely.

13. DON'T BOTHER WITH GADGETS

Or why to keep clear of so-called labour-saving devices

■■ ■■ ■■ ■■

"Never assume that the demonstrations you see carried out by skilled hands and trained eyes can be replicated in even the tiniest degree in your own home."

IT HAS been an otiose week in the howe. After nearly nine years in the house, we thought it would be an opportune moment last weekend to tidy out the garage. There had been word of a hitherto unknown tribe of pygmies inhabiting the back corner next to the heating boiler, so it seemed sensible to find out how they were all doing. We didn't find the pygmies, but we found all manner of junk that we had forgotten. How about the £70 cappuccino machine (Swiss-designed and German-made, the pinnacle of Teutonic engineering)?

This was something I bought in a mad moment at an Ideal Home show in 1992. I bought it because I had not yet learned the first principle of visiting exhibitions: buy nothing. Never assume that the demonstrations you see carried out by skilled hands and trained eyes in those controlled surroundings can be replicated in even the tiniest degree in your own home.

The delicious cup of cappuccino we enjoyed at the show stand at the Aberdeen Exhibition and Conference Centre was never more than hot dishwater at home. The machine made plenty racket and then would stop and fall silent.

It was that sort of silence that was long enough to make you worry and then, just as you approached the thing gingerly and began peering at its insides, it would bark, explode a column of steam and blow milk foam across half the kitchen.

We became convinced that the thing was demon-possessed, an impression not dulled by the way it rattled and shook its way across the worktop as it operated. Worse, it had to be cleaned thoroughly after every use. I don't mean just cleaned. I mean cleaned thoroughly. A dicht and a sweel were insufficient.

Unless you wanted the kitchen filled with the ripe aroma of sour milk for a couple of days, you had to unscrew at least four different parts, run a special brush through them and reassemble the thing. All for a cup of coffee.

You may take it that we were back on Nescafe pretty quickly and the machine was banished to the garage.

It was joined there over the succeeding years by various items, many of them which arrived at my desk unsolicited from companies looking for publicity. You would not believe how much junk arrives in a newspaper office from household names looking for a free plug.

As I write, there is a large pile, bound for a jumble sale, which includes a plastic Kellogg's iced-drink jug. The idea is that a central column in the jug will hold half a dozen ice cubes while you pour your juice into the part between the central column and the jug's outer surface.

This seems perfectly sound, even ingenious, except that our example's central column has no bottom to it. Thus, you drop the ice cubes in at the top and they land half a second later on your feet. This seems to be such an elementary design flaw in an ice jug that I was convinced for several minutes that I was missing something.

Then we have the ornamental cucumber preparer. I'm looking at the instruction leaflet as I write this. Depending on which blade you fit into the rather cheap plastic crank handle, you can make your cucumber into spirals, springs, laces, butterflies, melodeons, porcupines, half-moons and a dozen other knacky shapes, all to prettify your salads. And it works.

Here's the flaw. I don't like cucumber. I don't know anyone who likes cucumber.

Even if I liked cucumber, I imagine there would be a limit to how many cucumber melodeons I could polish off and still feel cheery. Off to the garage with that, too.

Then we have the toast stamp. This is a sort of vice that you're meant to clamp on to an edge of your kitchen worktop. When your toast pops out of your toaster, you transport it promptly to the toast stamp, line it up on the base plate and pull down the handle.

What do you get? You get a slice of toast that has the words "Good Morning" pressed into it.

I'm embarrassed enough admitting that such a device was given house room here and I hasten to add that I paid no money for it. It arrived in the Saturday mail and was retired to the garage on the Monday morning.

It could be, of course, that this ability to attract useless junk runs in the genes. I well remember the moment my father (or was it my mother?) succumbed to a TV advertisement in the early 1970s for the K-Tel Hair Stylist. "Save a fortune on your hairdressing bills. Become your own barber. Easy. Simple. £4.99. Ideal Christmas present."

When it arrived, it looked suspiciously like a comb with a long razor blade set into its teeth. According to the instruction manual, the best technique was to comb the hair as normal with firm, smooth and determined strokes.

Since my younger brother had immeasurably more sense, he volunteered to stand back and go second.

I sat on a stool in front of the fire, towel round my shoulders and, in a dozen "firm, smooth and determined strokes", saw enough hair land on my lap to stuff a couple of small scatter cushions.

To say that the results were haphazard would be to underplay K-Tel's achievement in flogging 3million of these things to other parents round Britain. I was a punk 10 years before Sid Vicious.

I had so many bald patches and tufts that I turned up at the academy assembly the following morning wearing my duffel-coat hood. I suffered the ignominy, in front of 500 fellow-pupils, of being told by the head teacher, calling brusquely from the platform: "That boy. You. Take off your hood at once. Height of bad manners."

And, under the gaze of a full hall, I had to reach up and peel back my coat hood and what was left of my dignity. They were decent enough not to laugh, but the gasp was a killer.

Then, also in the early 1970s, there was the K-Tel £2 17s 6d colour TV. Yes, £2 17s 6d.

This wasn't so much a TV as a sheet of tinted plastic for sticking on the front of the TV. The top third was dyed sky blue, the bottom third was dyed grass green and the middle was orange.

Presumably, this was on the basis that most outdoor shots consisted of sky at the top, grass at the bottom and something neutral in the centre.

I can tell you it didn't work particularly well even on outdoor shots, but it was bizarre whenever the cameras ventured inside. Every meal was green. All hair was blue. In close-up, every actor seemed to be stricken with the jandies. Our family bought a proper colour TV a couple of weeks later.

On reflection, I see our current garage clearout not as something to cause despair, but something to inspire pride. All this junk at my feet proves that I have been maintaining a family tradition.

None of these gadgets survives in our household now, although I do flick through Kaleidoscope brochures occasionally and, like small boys of all ages, I'm fascinated by sonar tape measures; toy parrots that repeat the last couple of words spoken to them, and motorised letter-openers — complete junk, but strangely compelling.

I'm not allowed to buy any of them.

14. HAPPY DAYS OF THE HALF-CROON

Or why pounds, shillings and pence were an enjoyable challenge

▬ ▬ ▬ ▬

"Had anyone set out to develop a monetary system to be as
complicated as possible, they could not have done a better
job than take Britain's LSD as the template."

IT HAS been a decimal week in the howe. This week in February, 2001, marks the 30th birthday of decimal coinage in the UK. It seems like only yesterday. Those of you who are 35 or younger have never known anything else, so it's almost impossible for you to believe that your elders managed to function with a system that operated not just to one mathematical base, but to two, side by side. Twelve pence to the shilling. Twenty shillings to the pound.

Had anyone set out actively to develop a monetary system to be as complicated as possible, they could not have done a better job than take Britain's LSD as the template.

It sounds like an arithmetical nightmare and probably was, but it was second nature to us. That was how we were taught in school, and the stuff you learn when you're young and impressionable never seems as daft as it really is.

Consider the following sum from Seven-a-Day, which was the standard Scottish textbook for mental arithmetic in the late 1960s:

You buy four pounds of potatoes at sixpence ha'penny a pound, three loaves at fivepence each and two bags of sugar at ninepence ha'penny each. How much change do you get from a 10-shilling note? You go home and you share your purchases with three

neighbours. How much does each of your neighbours have to pay you?

I'll give you the answers at the end, but no swicking. Take a moment to work it out honestly. I'll wait for you.

Never mind that you'll have a job splitting three loaves four ways, that was the sort of stuff we had to work out in our heads at age 10.

Daft or not, I still know several retired shop assistants who, with a little rehearsal to knock off the rust of 30 years, could glance down a column of old money and add it up, ha'penny perfect, in their heads. It's an impressive trick.

There are many theories about why this talent for an obscure monetary system should be so common among older Scots; most of them citing the rigours and excellence of the old Scottish educational system. I think it's more to do with the fact that very few of us in northern Scotland would willingly let a ha'penny escape.

You'll remember the excitement that decimalisation caused, very little of it positive. The publicity campaign began a year in advance, which seems remarkably lax in these days of three years' notice about a change of phone numbers in Coventry.

The Scaffold, that Liverpool trio, made a series of five-minute public-information films that were broadcast twice a day on BBC1 for weeks in advance until we were all sick of the sight of them.

Some of their advice seemed blindingly obvious, even at the time. They advised anyone likely to panicked by not having the exact money for any purchase to: "Give More, Get Change."

Yet all of that passed over those of us who were 13 and who were habitually mesmerised by anything new. We knew we were living through a moment of history because we could hardly have failed to notice all the media hysteria, but it was just a transient excitement to us.

I recall that the banks issued the coinage to the public a week in advance. It was an act of unmitigated cruelty. Millions of small boys were given money and told by law that they couldn't spend it.

Came the big day (a Monday, as I recall) and you couldn't see the academy for stue and sma steens when the 11am bell went. A sea of school uniforms thundered down into Market Place and we all queued up at the confectioners to spend this exciting new coin of the realm.

It was still the same old confectionery (Spangles, lucky tatties, Mojos, Love Hearts, coo candy), but the new coinage made it stirring somehow, and we hottered there like . . . well, like small boys in a sweetie shop.

In front of me stood a pupil who is now a major motor dealer in North-east Scotland. Behind me stood a pupil who is now a top orthopaedic surgeon. I was in the middle. Two successes out of three in one queue wasn't bad.

And we were all seized with the same hysteria; a delirium that would embarrass us now.

I wish I could report that the transition to new money was easy for the UK, but that would be lying. It didn't faze us teenagers, but many of our elders and betters took ill with it.

Newspaper letters columns were filled with angry dispatches from readers who felt that they couldn't respect a currency whose principal unit was apparently to be called a "pee".

One national tabloid began a campaign to have the name "pence" made compulsory in law, as if that would have made a blind bit of difference.

There were many such fears of change, but the only one that became fact was the fear of profiteering by companies who saw transitional confusion as a chance to rack up prices. I'm told by people who remember these things that a pint of beer cost 1s10d before decimalisation and 10p (two shillings) the night after. Within three years, it was 24p a pint (nearly five shillings).

A box of matches cost 3d the night before decimalisation and 2p (5d) within three weeks of the big day. A bag of crisps was 5d, but was up to 3p (7d) by Easter.

All sorts of lame excuses were trotted out by manufacturers for these rip-offs; the most patronising being that it was essential for public ease of use and understanding.

Some ventured that the new currency was less flexible because the minimum unit (half of one pence) was twice the value of the old minimum unit (ha'penny). Nobody was fooled by any of this chicanery, but they could do very little about it. Consumer power hadn't been invented yet. Consumer-protection legislation didn't exist. Watchdogs were things that took a chunk out of your leg if you strayed behind a 10ft fence after dark. Companies and stores had an open goal, knew it and aimed for it with the shameless drive of a parkful of Larssons.

For years after, many people did mental conversion back to old money, followed by the obligatory loud gasp, as in: "Forty-five pee for a packet of digestives? (Gasp.) That's *nine bob.*" I don't doubt that many masochists are still unable to shake the habit. "Seven bob for a pint of milk? I mind the days when . . ."

But all that profiteering is behind us now. Or is it? There's a little thing called the euro, which some people would ram down our throats to suit major exporters and Japanese-owned companies, but which anyone who remembers 1971 will know presents lucrative opportunities to the unscrupulous few. Thankfully, the national referendum will boot it out by at least three to one.

Besides, I still have sympathy for the old neighbour of ours in the howe who stared, dismayed, at a handful of small change in the week of decimalisation in 1971 and said sadly: "Could they nae hiv waitit or aa the aul fowk wis deid?"

The answers to the shopping sums are 2s2d for the potatoes, 1s3d for the bread and 1s7d for the sugar. The total is 5s, giving you change of 5s from the 10-bob note. Splitting the groceries with three neighbours would demand 1s3d from each of them.

> *I had a rash of letters pointing out a "mistake" in my calculations. But they had fallen into my trap for the unwary, similar to the traps laid by our teachers and exams. Details in the next column.*

15. RICH MELODY OF THE DORIC

Or why being bilingual is a matter of pride

■ ■ ■ ■

"The strength of the Doric is that its speakers are able to say in one word what might take a speaker of English an entire sentence to explain with equal colour and vigour."

IT HAS been a lexicographic week in the howe. You might have seen a feature series in one of the Sunday broadsheets about favourite words in English. The idea is that the newspaper features writer in charge of the series contacts the great and the good throughout the UK and asks them which word means most to them and which word they think sounds nicest.

An awful lot of it has been pretty humdrum fare. "Welcome" features a lot. So do "Love" and "Promotion". It's perhaps a sign of the times that one person thus far has tried to bend the rules by including a two-word phrase and nominating "I Quit" as the nicest-sounding.

The more compelling entries, however, are from the people you might expect: the celebrity writers and wits. Michael Palin nominated "Sandwich" as the word that meant most to him and, as the nicest-sounding, "Eleemosynary". As you'll know if you've been following our Wednesday adjectives, that means "relating to charity".

Stephen Fry thought the call of: "Waiter" meant most to him, while "Cheque" was the most melodious.

And so on and so on. You get the idea.

It set me to thinking about favourite words in the Doric. I hope our Highland and Island readers will excuse a little backyard reflection from this point. You're very welcome to stay.

The strength of the Doric, it has always seemed to me, is that its speakers are able to say in one word what a speaker of English, powerful and flexible a language though it is, would take a phrase or perhaps a sentence to explain with equal colour and vigour.

The point hit home a few weeks before Christmas when a colleague appeared at my desk and asked me to translate "throwe the bree".

I explained that when tatties or any other root vegetables were overboiled, their structure broke down and, if left long enough, they combined with the water in which they were boiling and became a watery mush.

A pained look crossed her face. "I ken that," she said, "but translate it into English. Do it in three words."

And I couldn't.

Try it. It's impossible to convey exactly the principle of "throwe the bree" in three English words.

That will always be the beauty and the strength of the Doric. The dialect is suffused with a colour and vigour that standard English cannot match so efficiently.

Try translating in one word exactly the qualities of wetness, greyness and chill that are inherent in "dreich". You can't.

So, we'll be generous. Try it in a sentence. You might manage it with considerable difficulty, but it won't be quite the same as just plain "dreich".

Doric draws at least half its strength from the fact that the sound of its words does half the work. It is, as the Principal Teacher of English at the academy never ceased reminding us, a rare example of a language that is almost entirely onomatopoeic.

Here's an example. In English, it's a child's toy trumpet. In Doric, it's a tooteroo. Even if you had no idea what a tooteroo was and couldn't even get a clue from the context, you'd make a reasonable stab at what the word meant just by saying it and listening to the sound.

In English, it's sweets. In Doric, it's gulshach. Say the word. Can't you hear every small boy who has ever had his mouth rammed so full of penny chews and liquorice straps that he can't talk for his mouth watering?

In English, it's to idle or loaf. In Doric, it's mollach. You can barely say the word without feeling sleepy.

It's almost impossible, given the inherent strength of the Doric, to pick five favourites, and I know you'll all have your own if you have any acquaintance with the dialect at all. For the moment, however, here are my top five.

At No.5, it's Dubs. Nothing conveys better the mixture of cloying, sucking and pervasive mud that is conveyed by the word Dubs. There's an element of excess and despair in Dubs that isn't apparent in plain ordinary English mud. Mud will dirty your shoes, but dubs will stop you in your tracks.

At No.4, it's Tyauve. Some people spell it Chaav, which apparently horrifies the Doric mafia, but since there's no long written tradition of Doric, just you carry on spelling it how you like. It means long, pained and wearying labour however you spell it.

Say Tyauve properly, with the long drawn-out vowels of rural Aberdeenshire and Banffshire, and your back begins to ache, you feel like a seat and maybe a good hot bath to ease away the strains of the day. It's a word that really works for its living.

At No.3, it's Swick. You can be exploited, cheated or led up the garden path, but there's little quite so annoying as being swickit, because the implication is that you should have seen through an easy deception. Note that the deception itself is "a swick" and that the perpetrator, too, is "a swick".

At No.2, it's Blaad, meaning to spoil something. How many times were people of my vintage and older given birthday or Christmas presents and warned gravely: "Dinna blaad it."?

But the top Doric word in my book is (pause, open gold envelope) . . .

. . . contermacious. There are difficult people. There are obstinate people. There are un-cooperative people. But none of those is so downright irritating as someone who's contermacious.

A contermacious person is difficult just for the sake of it. Black is white to a contermacious person, and white is black. If a contermacious person sees an opportunity to stick a spoke in someone's wheel, he'll do it and take a quiet pleasure in it. If a contermacious person is presented with an opportunity to do someone else a kindness, guess what? And there are more of these people about than you think.

But that's contermacious, the meatiest Doric word of the lot.

Jot down your own top five if you have a moment and drop me a line. It's always interesting to compare notes.

FINALLY, a postscript to last week's column on decimalisation. You might remember that I included a shopping sum in pounds, shillings and pence to test your skills with old money.

I won't trouble you with it all again, except to say that the last part invited you to divide your five bob's worth of messages with three neighbours and asked how much each neighbour would owe you. The answer was 1s3d.

Several of you called, wrote or faxed to chide me gently, pointing out that dividing five bob's worth of groceries with three neighbours surely would demand 1s8d from each.

I'm sorry to be picky, but by dividing the messages with three neighbours, you're sharing things four ways, including yourself. The answer remains 1s3d. I tried to give you a clue by making a joke about the difficulty of splitting three loaves four ways.

Had you been dividing the groceries "among" three neighbours, then 1s8d would have been right.

And had you been in my primary-school class, you'd have been across teacher's knee by now, being told with each whack: "You — Must — Read — The — Question — Carefully."

I wasn't expecting the mailbag that followed this one . . .

16. YOUR FAVOURITE DORIC WORD

Or why there's no chance that our language will die

▬ ▬ ▬ ▬

"I don't think my mail has been heavier in the last 20 years. They came by post and by fax. There were phone calls, e-mails and people stopping me in the street."

IT HAS been an enchorial week in the howe. The request last week for your Top Five Doric words certainly seemed to strike a chord (or should that be "tak a trick")?

I don't think my mail has been heavier in the last 20 years. They came as a small mountain by post and by fax. There were several phone calls and several dozen e-mails. I had people stopping me in the street, standing at my desk and waylaying me in the corridors.

I'll admit to being quite tickled that there is still such phenomenal interest in the dialect — and not just from older readers, either.

Usually, the people who stopped to chat would remind me that I had asked for contributions before listing their own favourites. Occasionally, I would hear a single word shouted from the far end of a room or a lobby, followed by a wave and a grin. In most places where I have ventured in the past week, I've become used to hearing a chorus of: "Spurtle", "Hoast", "Nickum" and "Sotter".

I was standing in the queue in the Lang Stracht canteen when one of the advertising ladies walked past and said: "Gutsy", which I preferred to take as a contribution to our Doric opinion poll, rather than as a comment relating to my heaped plate of skirlie and tatties. One afternoon, I looked up to find a colleague from one of our many district offices standing there. All he said was: "Gommerel" which, if you know Banffshire Doric at all, could have been a personal slight.

But it was the response from you, the public, that was most rewarding, and I'm still working my way through them, so what you're going to get here is a selection from the top three-quarters of the pile. I've respected the wishes of people who have asked for anonymity, although I'm sure there's nothing to be shy about in loving your language.

The principal surprise was that one particular Doric word featured somewhere in the lists of almost two-thirds of the readers who contributed so, clearly, that must be the North-east's favourite Doric word. I'll keep you guessing for a wee while yet.

For top value, Flora Davidson, of Westhill, offered not a Top Five but a Top 12. She claimed she "nivver wis tap at coontin at Clatt Public School durin the waar". Among Flora's were fusionless (worn out), sipin (soaked), soor beukey (indigestion), connacht (broken), clortit (dirty) and . . . the North-east's favourite Doric word.

Forbes Grant, of Banchory, offered pyocher (congestion), raivelt (confused), yarkit (burdened to excess), snorrel (disorganisation) and connacht.

Frances Jaffray, of Ellon, favoured scunner (bore), sharger (the runt of the litter) and . . . the North-east's favourite Doric word.

A reader from Dingwall, who is clearly an exile from the North-east, suggested pyochrin (coughing), hyterin (stumbling), sklytered (covered in dirt) and . . . the North-east's favourite Doric word.

Mary Munro, of Ballater, offered an anecdote from her days as a primary teacher at Monymusk, when pupils were required to stand in front of the class and give a short speech on something that interested them. One boy, a son of the soil, decided on an explanation of his farm chores.

At one point, he explained that he was required regularly to "clear the skitter" from the byre. A mystified fellow-pupil, newly arrived from Down South, put up her hand and inquired as to what "skitter" might be. The orator struggled bravely to translate the Doric into accurate English, then brightened and said: "Weet diarrhoea."

Mrs Munro went on to list as her favourites gorbellt (an egg with the young bird formed inside), fykie (fiddly and difficult, as in an intricate task), connacht, heepocondriach (which sounds like hypochondriac, but means depressed or listless) and . . . the North-east's favourite Doric word.

Elma Fowlie, of Oldmeldrum, favours huddery (unkempt and untidy, as in a woman's perm going wrong, resulting in her being "huddery-heidit for a file"), pernickety (precise), wisgan (a twerp — Elma went on to cite Robin Cook as an example) and . . . the North-east's favourite Doric word.

Elma also had a tale from just after the war, when her husband went into a shop at New Deer which sold everything from agricultural implements to sweeties (gulshach). Behind the counter was an extremely elderly gentleman who had been summoned out of retirement to cover while the men were away in the Forces.

"Hiv ye ony graips?" asked young Fowlie.

The old man fixed him with a look and said: "Muck or aetin?"

A couple from Glen Tanar, on Deeside, offered His and Hers Top Fives. The "Hers" were clort (dirt, an oaf or to smear), feerich (simmering with excitement), fow (to toss straw or to kick the feet idly), skitter and guff. The "His" were scunner (to sicken, bore or irritate), lippen (to trust), stravaigin (exploring and roaming boldly), trauchled (worn out and burdened) and . . . the North-east's favourite Doric word.

Grace Shaw, of Forres, offered stappit fu (packed to excess), scraich (a wail or screech), sooch (a breeze; used most often in "keeping a calm sooch", meaning to stay level-headed) and . . . the North-east's favourite Doric word.

Harry Innes, of Turriff, said he started several lists, but had great difficulty getting it down to just five. Eventually, he thought we'd excuse six and plumped for dottled (confused, usually applied to older people), mochey (which can mean either grey and drizzly or baking hot, believe it or not), cummat (upset), vrocht (worked), lowsin (ending the day's labours) and . . . the North-east's favourite Doric word.

A Foggieloan reader favoured fashious (fretful and difficult, usually of children), ill-fashience (nosiness), fyachie (a dull and sickly colour, usually accompanied by "broon" to describe an unattractive shade of paint or an unappetising soup), kirn (an unappealing mixture, often culinary) and . . . the North-east's favourite Doric word.

Which brings me, I suppose, to the moment you've been waiting for. Which is the clear favourite in the North-east Doric lexicon?

Before I tell you, I'll thank everyone who wrote, faxed, phoned or e-mailed me. There are too many of you for me to write to you individually, but I'm delighted that you took the time and trouble. I've not been able to mention everyone here, but I'm reading and enjoying all your letters.

So, without further ado, I can tell you that the North-east's favourite word in the Doric is . . . (drum roll, pause, open gold envelope) . . .

. . . ferfochen.

And you really don't need me to tell you what that means.

At the time of writing this book, nine months after the two Doric columns appeared, I'm still getting lists of Doric from throughout the Commonwealth.

Who said the Doric was dying?

By the way, several readers did write to ask what ferfochen meant. Just for the record, it means "exhausted" and "cheesed off" in equal measure. You can also spell it forfochen.

17. COURAGE OF AN UNSUNG HERO

Or why not to assume that humble men can't be great

▬ ▬ ▬ ▬

*"For conspicuous valour against overwhelming odds in
the Crimean War, John Perie became one of the
North-east's very few holders of the Victoria Cross."*

IT HAS been a dreadnought week in the howe. Today, I want
to tell you a story that has been lost in the mists of history for
far too long. It concerns the obscurity of humble beginnings,
rising to the national fame which attends all great acts of courage.
It's a tale of a man who thought little of himself, but acted
selflessly for others. Sadly, it's also a tale which ends in a manner
that such a man didn't deserve.

This is the story of John Perie.

John was born to a family at Gartly, five miles south of Huntly
on the Rhynie road, in 1821. Like most rural North-east families of
the time, they were dirt poor. Education passed John by. He could
neither read nor write, but he could certainly work hard and
found labouring jobs in the area to help keep the family solvent.

The family name wasn't Perie at all. They were Pirries, a
common enough name in the southern part of Strathbogie at the
time, always with two Rs and always pronounced Peerie.

When John signed up with the Royal Artillery in Aberdeen
shortly after New Year 1848, the recruiting sergeant asked for his
name. "Peerie," he said, and was duly entered in the register as
John Perie.

He transferred to the Corps of Sappers and Miners and served in

Gibraltar and Turkey before being sent to the hotspot of the mid-19th century, the Crimean War. That was where John's national fame became assured.

In the early-morning darkness of June 18, 1855, in the hills behind Sebastopol on the Black Sea coast, British units gathered for an assault on the last Russian makeshift fort, known as a redan. Success meant taking a key position for a final assault on Sebastopol. Failure would result in heavy casualties.

John was selected as the sapper to lead one party of sailors carrying ladders. The idea was to prop the ladders against the redan walls in the darkness, then pour troops up and inside. It seems almost suicidal now. Indeed, that was how it turned out.

The hoped-for element of surprise was no surprise at all. As soon as the order to attack was given, Russian fire was constant and merciless. British troops fell in horrendous numbers without even reaching the redan walls.

The ladder parties reached a forward trench and took cover. When Russian fire died down after 10 minutes, they tried again. The results were no better the second time. Given that death must have seemed certain, the courage of these ladder-carrying sailors, and of John Perie, who guided them, now seems extraordinary.

In any case, they were forced to retreat to the trench once again. By this point, it was clear that the plan was futile, so it was called off. Once the noise of battle had faded, and the men were gathering their strength and dealing with their trauma, one officer heard the groan of a wounded ladder-party sailor out on the exposed ground.

He called for volunteers to join him on a rescue attempt. A Lt. Gerald Graham cried: "I'm with you." Then a third figure scrambled forward, saying: "And me." It was John Perie.

The three men went over the top, taking great risks considering that daybreak was beginning to creep from behind the hills. They located the wounded man in a terrible scatter of British bodies and hauled him back to safety.

Unknown to the two officers at the time, Perie had been wounded severely in the side by Russian musket shot in either the first or second ladder attack, but hadn't thought to mention it.

For conspicuous valour in twice leading the ladder-party sailors against overwhelming odds, and for helping rescue a wounded man despite being severely wounded himself, John Perie became one of the North-east's very few recipients of the Victoria Cross. Even now, at almost 150 years' remove, that's quite an achievement for a fairm loon from Gartly who couldn't read or write.

He was hospitalised and returned to London for surgery. While there, he was presented to Queen Victoria, who pinned the medal on his chest.

John discharged himself from the Army in 1860, forfeited his claim to a service pension for some reason, and headed for home on the train.

There's a tale that he got wind of a civic reception awaiting him at the Joint Station in Aberdeen so, being self-effacing and probably not a little thrawn, he got off the train at Stonehaven. There's no proof that that actually happened.

John's decline from then was steady. Like many former soldiers of his day, he found solace in the bottle. He and his daughters had a small shop in East North Street, Aberdeen, but whether by misfortune or abuse, John died near-destitute in the autumn of 1874. He was buried at St Peter's Cemetery, off King Street, in a pauper's grave shared on the same day with 12 others.

No headstone commemorated his bravery. No newspaper recorded the passing of a man whose valour and gallantry reflected so well on his home airt.

And that might have been that.

Then, a century later, David Harvey, a young Metropolitan Police officer, visited Highgate Cemetery in London and, as he strolled along the stones, spotted the grave of a VC winner and wondered how many other such graves he might be able to visit. It became his life's hobby and took him worldwide.

During his researches between trips, he was astonished and horrified to discover that the last resting places of about 1700 of these brave men had gone unrecorded, and set about trying to put that right.

In Aberdeen, former Royal Engineer Douglas Mitchell and Col

Ian McAdam, began researching the life of John Perie and locating the grave.

The upshot is that after more than a year of painstaking work, the North-east will put right its oversight of the life of one of its bravest sons when a commemorative headstone is unveiled in a formal ceremony at St Peter's. Douglas Mitchell and Ian McAdam will see the fruits of their interest and their work put right a serious omission that lasted for almost a century and a half.

The stone will not stand over Perie's grave, because that remains a mass lair and marking that would not be appropriate given that 12 other poor souls lie there with him. However, it will be placed in a prominent spot near the cemetery gates. Douglas Mitchell and Ian McAdam hope to have city and military representatives there to give the ceremony the dignity and respect that John Perie deserves.

In case you're wondering, the medal lies in the regimental museum at Chatham, bought for a little more than £60 in 1911 by a firm in Piccadilly. It sits with John Perie's other honours, including the Crimea Medal with four clasps, the French Medal of Valour and the Turkish Crimea Medal.

It transpires now that the Army had never forgotten Perie, even although the North-east had. The Engineers still have a Perie Day, when the newest recruit attends a regimental dinner and sits at the right hand of the commanding officer. There is a particular style of barrack block known as Perie blocks. He also has a street named after him, and few sons of Gartly can claim that.

But, then, few sons of anywhere have been able to claim such tangible proof of their courage under fire and their selfless thought for their colleagues.

━━ ━━ ━━ ━━

The oversight was put right at last on June 17, 2001

18. JOYS OF LIFE IN THE CLASSROOM

Or how to cope if you (or your spouse) is a teacher

■■ ■■ ■■ ■■

"I am married to a teacher. Teachers frequently forget
when they are in front of a class and when they are at
home in the bosom of their families."

I T HAS been an idoneous week in the howe. From time to time, there are hazards about writing columns in which the brief is, basically, to talk about yourself. What a thoroughly unnatural way to make a living, but that is specifically what a personal columnist is paid to do.

This turn of career has amused my family more than somewhat in the past 14 years, since they know that in real life, not in the two-dimensional, 1,150-word world of newsprint, I am what you might call extremely reserved and private. I can think of little more enjoyable than a day by myself, and little more daunting than a social event full of strangers.

Blasting my personal life across half of Scotland to a third of a million readers once a week wouldn't have been the obvious line of work, then. It's akin to people with a fear of heights taking up tightrope-walking, or herpetophobes becoming snake-charmers.

But there are rewards, and the reward in writing columns comes not in seeing your ugly mug in print twice a week, as some people assume, because the novelty of that passes very quickly. The reward comes in the mailbag that arrives the following day.

Whether the response is good or bad, appreciative, chiding or absolutely furious, it's always interesting to realise that wildly different things have been inferred from exactly the same 1,150 words. Even now, I can never predict how any single column will be received. No columnist can. In that respect, I'm still learning.

But of all the responses that have come my way in the last 14 years, there is one mystifying message that arises time and again, in notes, faxes, e-mails, phone calls and, from bolder readers, to my face.

It is this:

"You're awful hard on Mrs Harper."

We've been out dining quietly and acquaintances have come up to our table. I have introduced her to them and, often, at least one will say to her something like: "My goodness, you must have a thick skin."

"He must be quite a challenge," is a close second.

"How on earth do you put up with it?" is another, and I catch her basking in this thoroughly unjustified outpouring of needless sympathy.

I have often cast my mind back over past columns wondering where and how I might have given this false impression of a burdened, stoical and long-suffering wife. Each time, the answer is the same: canna see't masel.

She is married to a quiet soul who makes his living sitting in a corner at a computer keyboard not bothering anybody. I am married to a teacher. Teachers frequently forget when they are in front of a class and when they are at home in the bosoms of their families. I know shopkeepers who can tell instantly whether or not the person they are serving is a teacher, just by that person's manner.

Which one of us deserves the sympathy?

Those of you whose wives teach know what I mean. You're able to tell, by the speed of her car arriving at the end of the day, and the tone of the car door shutting, if it's been a good, not-so-good or downright awful day at the office.

You have seen your wife demonstrate her prime qualification for teaching teenagers: the skill of gulping down a full lunch in three minutes and 14 seconds, then abandoning you to hare off and tackle some unseen emergency.

You know that she has developed an eerie skill of knowing whether or not it's a full moon without even looking outside.

You know the difficulty you had in naming your children, because there wasn't a single name in the entire English language that didn't bring on high blood pressure the moment she heard it uttered.

It's very difficult for a teacher to unburden herself of her daily cares at home. Professional ethics mean that she can't discuss many of the day's events for fear of breaking the teacher-pupil-parent confidence pact.

Find yourself at a social function full of teachers and it's exactly the same, only multiplied dozens of times over. I've heard tales of one Aberdeenshire school where the head teacher was having the staff room remodelled and thought it would be a democratic idea to consult the staff on what (affordable) new fixtures they might like to see included.

He pinned a blank sheet of paper on the staff notice board seeking ideas. The following morning, a hasty scribble had requested a Valium salt lick.

At another, a sub-committee was set up to discuss redesigning the report cards sent home for first, second and third-year pupils. One of the committee members suggested there should be tick-box for "shallow gene pool".

One of my old teachers, I discovered only recently, used to keep himself sane by compiling a scrapbook of parental letters. Among them, I'm led to believe, is one that ran something like:

"Please excuse Jeannie from not being at the school yesterday. We thought it was Sunday because the paper boy didn't deliver the daily paper. It was only when the paper-shop man delivered the paper himself in the afternoon, and we saw it was the Press and Journal, not the Sunday Post, that we realised our mistake."

Another was: "Dear Mr B-----, I'm terribly sorry that Alan was late for the school yesterday. He's an awful heavy sleeper. I forgot to wake him up and I didn't find him until I started making the beds."

But occasionally, teachers come home, their little faces beaming, and you just know that something has tickled them that day, or some struggling pupil has finally broken through and achieved something that had seemed beyond reach for so long, and you know that they've had their professional reward, too.

Not so long ago, just before the Easter holidays, Mrs Harper met up with an old colleague who had retrained and was just past the half-way mark of her first year as head teacher of a smallish rural North-east primary. She had been filling in for the Primary Seven teacher who was off sick and, as is the way with emergency stand-ins, had had to concoct a lesson out of nothing.

She thought she would have an impromptu quiz on proverbs and sayings, which involved giving the class the first half of a proverb and asking them to complete it. That might have been second nature to people of my vintage or older, but proverbs aren't exactly the staple fare of modern 10-year-olds.

She said she started the lesson hoping that it wasn't going to be too boring and finished it scarcely able to stay composed. As soon as the class finished, she raced to her room to jot down some of the offerings, including:

"A penny saved is . . . not much."

"Too many cooks . . . are not good if your kitchen is small."

"Empty barrels . . . are affa easy coupit."

"A rolling stone . . . can dent your car."

"Children should be seen and not . . . smacked."

"Laugh and the world laughs with you. Cry and you . . . have to blow your nose."

I found several kindred spirits after this one. It seems that off-duty teachers have similar habits, and that non-teaching husbands (and wives) have to cope as best they can.

19. ROBBED OF LIFE BY CRUELLEST DISEASE

Or why dementia patients and families bear an immense burden

*"We who are left behind while the victim's world closes
about him have no means of knowing what
to do, what to say or how to cope."*

IT HAS been a successive week in the howe. I wish I could promise that today will offer some of the usual whimsy to lighten your Wednesday, but I can't say that I'm feeling especially whimsical.

As part of our recent holiday, we ventured to visit a relative at her home in the Highlands. We hadn't seen her in nine months, which was too long a lapse and which needed to be put right. More important, we hadn't seen her husband in nearly four years since he had been admitted to a nursing home, suffering from the early stages of dementia. It felt proper to put right that sorry omission, too.

What can I tell you? Four years is a long time not to see the lively, funny and brosey man who was simply a wee bit forgetful the last time we met. Now, he is immobile, unrecognising and lives from bed to wheelchair to bed to wheelchair. I confess I came away with a sair hert.

I'm not going to labour the specifics, because his illness is a private matter, but any of you who have a loved one suffering from Alzheimer's Disease, or who can recall trying vainly to cope with the intensely demanding nature of their illness, will know.

He's not the first family member to suffer from dementia. My grandfather died in hospital in 1983, but I was younger then and, selfishly, did not see my own mortality in quite such sharp focus.

Nevertheless, it was immensely distressing for a grandson to stand in a hospital room, behind a locked door, and watch the grandfather he always respected and admired lying curled up in an institutional bed and crying out, with the pain of a wounded beast, for his wife who had died 18 years before. The image haunts me still.

I remember feeling the need to try to calm him so, more by way of conversation than question, I said: "Do you miss her?"

He fell into floods of uncontrollable sobbing and I had to get myself from the room.

One of the cruellest things about Alzheimer's is that there is no rationality about it. We who are left behind while the victim's world closes about him have no means of knowing what to do, what to say or how to cope.

Relatives of sufferers tell stories which follow remarkably similar courses. All of them report that it begins with amusement at the person's forgetfulness, clumsiness or occasional senseless chatter. Even the victim is amused. They are amused, rather than alarmed, because there is no inkling of the chasm that lies ahead.

Then comes frustration that the person seems unwilling to make an effort to mend his ways. Then comes irritation, which is usually when the doctor is called and the diagnosis begins. This gives way quickly to anger: anger that this despicable condition should be visited on an otherwise vital and hearty person. Then comes despair as the demands increase, followed by the guilt when it becomes apparent that professional care is the best way forward, then the resignation that there is unlikely to be much hope.

The greatest of these, I'm told, is the guilt. Once a patient is hospitalised, many families torture themselves with thoughts that they could and should have done more, or that they could or should be doing more. Yet it is irrational to believe that committing a loved one to professional care is selfish and abandoning.

The proper perspective is that it is almost always an act of great charity for both parties.

I hadn't been in a dementia ward for nearly two decades, but the basics have not changed much. Anyone with even a passing familiarity with the condition can see the various stages of the disease being played out before them.

There are the patients who seem lucid and bright and who can still hold a decent conversation. There are the ones who sit, smiling and nodding, but saying little or nothing. There are the ones who walk purposefully, but blankly, up and down the corridors, back and forth across dayrooms in endless, tormented strolls. There are the ones sitting in their wheelchairs, surrounded by their relatives. And there are the screams from distant bedrooms.

It would take an iron constitution not to be moved by all of this.

Sit there watching, and it is impossible not to ponder that every one of these lost souls was once an inquisitive child, a hearty teenager, a vibrant young man or woman, a loving husband or wife, mother or father.

Look at the resigned smiles offered by other visiting relatives, each one of them knowing exactly what every other visitor is thinking and bearing. There's a weary, but supportive communion about these places.

A former colleague told me that two thoughts troubled him most. The first was that in his despair he was feeling sorry for himself, when he should have been feeling sorry for his sister. This is a question most Alzheimer's relatives deal with regularly.

They comfort themselves with the thought that the longer-term patients are usually unaware of anything that is happening to them, callous though that might sound. Visit one of these homes and it is easy to see the truth in it.

But that brought him to his second worry, he said: his sister's occasional, momentary flashes of lucidity in weeks upon weeks of blankness. "They're the moments that really trouble me," he said, "because that's when you confront the most torturing thought of all: how much might she be knowing and hearing and feeling and thinking, but is trapped there, screaming inside?

"All the medical advice to the contrary is logical, but I just can't cope with those moments at all. And that's when I get back to thinking whether or not I'm feeling sorrier for myself than for my sister. It's a vicious circle I would never wish on anyone."

It would be very easy to leave one of these homes or hospitals wondering what on earth the point of it all was; that life wasn't meant to peter out so cruelly. It's an awful thought, I know, but I couldn't help thinking it for hours afterwards.

The one cheering thought, apart from the fact that research is powering ahead in several Western countries, is remembering the hospital and home staff. I know nursing homes get more of a bad press than a good one; the rotten apples in every professional barrel tarnish the reputations of the majority.

I can tell you only from my recent experience that these people demonstrate care and patience that I could never dream of matching. The comfort in all of this is that your relative is in such good hands.

But it would be fine, wouldn't it, if our loved ones could be restored to us as we always knew them, and they always knew us, and they had no need to be in any hands at all?

This column drew one of the most touching mailbags of 2001. An immense amount of despair and sadness affects so many families throughout North and North-east Scotland.

Happily, many correspondents were able to be remarkably positive in their outlook. Although they accepted that there was unlikely to be much progress in fighting the condition in time to help their own families, they hoped that research continued so that others needn't suffer in future what was being suffered in the present.

20. NOTHING UP MY SLEEVE

Or why bad magicians can be more entertaining than good ones

■■■ ■■ ■■■ ■■■

"Table magic, as it's called, involves playing cards,
hankies, cups and balls. It's magic at its most demanding
because it's being performed right under your nose."

IT HAS been a prestidigitationary week in the howe. If you're familiar at all with corporate dinners, those events by which companies or organisations say thank-you to past clients and try to seduce potential future trade, you'll be familiar with the concept of the after-dinner entertainment.

This can take many forms. Usually, it's a humorous speech, but sometimes it's a musical ensemble plinking and plunking in the background, competing with the clink of glasses, the champing of jaws and the scraping of cutlery on china. Sometimes it's a cabaret singer.

And sometimes it's magic.

The renaissance of the illusionist as corporate entertainment is a growing trend, mainly because the available pool of good after-dinner speakers is surprisingly small in Scotland. So the Magic Circle has a list of conjurers; men and women whose day jobs vary from van-drivers to professors, but who at night become practitioners of the twin black arts of illusion and deception; people who are willing to try to astound half-cut dinner guests in return for a handsome fee.

I've been to three such dinners in the past year. One magician was astonishingly good. His was the sort of magic which was far more impressive than the TV stuff in which articulated lorries disappear in the middle of the street and voluptuous assistant Sadie-Jo materialises in her swimsuit inside a large block of ice.

Table magic, as it's called, involves playing cards, hankies, cups and balls, and seems much tamer until you witness it being performed well. It's magic at its most demanding because it's being done right under your nose where, theoretically, you can spot the sleight of hand.

Well, you can't.

At least, you can't if it's done properly.

The best of the three was an American. I forget his name, but I saw him at a dinner in Tayside in the company of about 20 other guests. The climax to his act was producing 24 forks and knives from various pockets in the jacket of one of my colleagues. To this day, my journalist friend doesn't know how it happened. He felt no weight in his jacket. He felt no sensation of the cutlery being transferred from the magician to him before being "found" seconds later. There appeared to be no discernible jiggery-pokery.

That's my friend's story, of course. For three months, he has had his leg pulled that his attempt to steal a canteen of cutlery for his wife's birthday was rumbled at the last minute.

The second magician appeared at a dinner in Aberdeen. I think he was an assistant rector of a secondary school and his bearing and appearance were the most impressive. He was dressed impeccably in his dinner jacket and dicky-bow, and his dexterity with cards and styrofoam balls was mesmerising.

Even when we cynics decided that we'd concentrate not on the hand doing all the business, as clearly the conjurer wanted, but on the hand that was always hovering around one or another of his pockets, still not one of us could tell how he was pulling off such consummate visual trickery.

Foam balls would disappear from diners' tightly clenched fists and reappear in other diners' wallets. Yes, I know they'll have been different balls, but how he did it was beyond us.

Our signatures on playing cards would appear inside sealed envelopes in women guests' handbags.

He would borrow a watch from one of us, lock it inside a box, then ask another guest, a stranger to him, to name any time of day. When he opened the box again, the watch would be set to that exact time.

It's seeing people as good as these two magicians that swears you off trying your hand at Find The Lady in fairground stalls. Don't even think about it. You haven't a hope of anything except losing your money.

Good as these two were, it was the third one who was most entertaining, for all the wrong reasons. He was the oldest of the three. His dinner jacket was a hire job, and so ill-fitting that we wondered in the beginning if he was a comic magician in the Tommy Cooper mould.

He was certainly well past retiring age and bore a perpetual sadness, which didn't exactly put the wind at his back if he was contemplating a career as an after-dinner entertainer.

His ploy was to perform not after the dinner to the entire assembly, but to drift from table to table during the meal and perform small tricks under our noses. He appeared at our table during the main course and fixed on Alan as his likeliest dupe.

As Alan stood up, his chair moved back sharply, knocking the magician's leg. A pack of playing cards fell from somewhere inside the magician's voluminous jacket and landed in a scatter at his feet.

We all laughed, thinking this was the act ice-breaker, but I could tell by the way he wasn't reacting to the laughter, but was staring horrified and panic-stricken at the scatter of cards, that the accident was genuine and had put paid to at least five minutes of his act.

He struggled on gamefully. He tried misdirecting Alan's attention while trying to swipe Alan's watch. He fumbled it so badly that Alan noticed, clapped a hand over the watch and said: "No, you don't."

He tried a foam-ball transference trick, but it was spoiled when the guests pointed out that the disappeared ball had been green, while the reappeared ball was yellow.

Throughout his act, something was moving inside his jacket. One of my fellow-guests said later that he had been tempted, just for fun, to hit it, but had been terrified that there would be a pained squawk and a puff of feathers.

Every trick this poor man tried went wrong in some way. When we had passed the stage of believing that this was comedy magic, but had realised instead that it was just incompetence, that hot feeling of embarrassment descended over us. We were all staring at our plates, willing him to stop for his own sake.

The two women at the table came over all motherly, despite the fact that he was old enough to be their grandfather. They would point out helpfully where the hidden card might be. "Not there? What about that pocket?" That must only have compounded his misery.

Who but the British would be so encouraging to a complete failure?

Trouper to the last, he finished this 12-minute set with a bow, which sent a wristwatch tumbling from his breast pocket, and a closing line which will be impossible to forget: "Thank you, ladies and gentlemen, you've been a great audience."

And off he limped to a side room, the clank of concealed metal rings accompanying every step, where presumably he intended to feed his doo.

I've since seen the middle magician again. This time, he performed a levitation trick on a woman guest at a corporate dinner. She swears that she has no idea how it was done. She felt nothing. There was no collusion. She simply had a sensation of floating and a numbness about her neck. She says she's thankful he didn't try cutting her in half.

21. DEAR SIR, YOURS SINCERELY

Or how to get your views published in a newspaper

▬ ▬ ▬ ▬

*"A newspaper that doesn't foster a spirited exchange of
views with its customers or give them a platform to express
opinions is a pretty limp publication altogether."*

IT HAS been a correspondential week in the howe. I've been
pondering. What's the most important page in a newspaper?
It's not mine, much as I might wish it. I'm aware of a
columnist's relative importance in the machine.

Is it the front page, then, containing all the breaking news and
showcasing the paper as it lies on the newsagent's counter, luring
casual customers into an impulse buy? Or the TV page; the one
most people read every day (94% of you)? Maybe, it's the page
reader surveys rate most highly: the local news on Page Three.

Perhaps, as journalists suspect in our despairing moments, it's
the Births, Marriages and Deaths. Or perhaps it doesn't really
matter which is most important as long as newsprint can still be
torn into a pile of small squares with a string through the corner.

I don't think any of the obvious candidates can lay claim to top
spot. The most important page in the Press and Journal — or any
newspaper — is the page that carries the readers' letters.

A newspaper that doesn't foster a spirited exchange of views
with its customers or give them a platform to express opinions that
wouldn't be heard otherwise is a limp publication altogether.

That's why we will always encourage you to get out the writing
pad and vent your spleen on any and every issue of the day.

95

You have to understand one thing before we go any further, though: we receive far more letters each day than we have a hope of publishing. In that arithmetical truth lies a diplomatic minefield for every Letters Editor. The many who do not make the cut assume that it's because we think their opinions are worthless, or that they are being censored, or that the Press and Journal is frightened of upsetting an advertiser.

Some unsuccessful correspondents are not shy of phoning up and throwing tantrums to that effect. Our hapless letters sub-editor explains with great patience that there simply wasn't the room.

This brings us to the second difficulty with readers' letters: the many and wondrous ways some correspondents will try to bend the rules. The least sophisticated are political parties before an election. Every one of them marshals its faithful to try to pass off propaganda as genuine readers' letters. One party is particularly blatant, seemingly unaware that letters editors see the same prescribed phrases in missive after missive and put the lot straight in the No file. Readers' letters pages are for readers, not political broadcasts.

Some councillors see the page as a soapbox for telling constituents how wonderful and hard-working they are. The contortions in these letters are admirable as their writers try to spin them as newsworthy, but carry a shameless plug at the same time.

"SIR, — Like Mr Farquhar, I was upset that our swimming pool has had to close for repairs so soon, but as the person who was instrumental in having the whole thing built, marshalling the tireless efforts of a team for the long-term benefit of our wonderful community . . ." You get the idea.

Some correspondents want to make the bullets then have the Press and Journal fire them as they hide behind that handy device: Name and Address Supplied. Plenty of newspapers do this, but the Press and Journal's policy is that people with an opinion need to have the courage of their convictions and stand by them openly, however uncomfortable. It's the responsibility that goes with the privilege of free speech.

Only in exceptional circumstances does that rule lapse; perhaps not more than a dozen times a year. The last one I can think of was a mother in her 30s who had had a secret abortion at the age of 17 and who wanted to deplore a particular politician's clod-headed views on the subject. Obviously, the woman's view was poignant and pertinent, but she was entitled to privacy, too.

We have correspondents who try the false-name or false-address gambits, unaware that each letter from an unfamiliar address is checked out. The most memorable recent occurrence was a Deeside reader who wanted to complain about plans to build a retail centre on the Aberdeen side of Banchory, but who was such a feartie that he (or she) used the name and address of one of the town ministers, to the minister's great bemusement when we checked with him.

We have businesses who think the page is an opportunity for a free advertisement, again on the pretext of responding to a previous item. "SIR, — I was saddened to read of Mr Jamieson's problems (the Press and Journal, August 10) with his neighbour's dog barking through the night. It seems to me that a course of canine aromatherapy is needed. I have tried this with our own Chihuahua-Great Dane cross and it worked a treat. So much so that I have now become a registered canine aromatherapist, recognised by the Canine Aromatherapy Council of Great Britain. Special rates for pensioners. Visa and Mastercard accepted."

We have correspondents who want to have an argument in print. Mr A's views are published. Mr B writes to dispute the views. Mr A writes to say that Mr B is evidently a profound neep. Mr B says there was no need for that, and if anyone is a neep, it's Mr A. Nowadays, these last-word exchanges are stopped sooner.

In my greener days in the late 1980s, when I was responsible for the Letters content, we had a reader at Inverness and one at Nairn who couldn't stand each other and who wanted to bicker in print every week. Nowadays, I'd be more diplomatic, but then, after a dozen such exchanges, I wrote each a letter containing the other one's phone number and suggested they gave each other a call. The letters stopped, as probably did two daily sales of the paper.

And sometimes, we get calls from readers who want to know why their letter hasn't been published, yet "Mr So-and-so appears in the Letters Page almost every week".

That would be because Mr So-and-so, any of our regulars whose names most of you will recognise, has learned the knack.

1. Keep it short: fewer than 100 words if you can. The most we can publish is 250 words if we are to give a chance to as many people as possible.

2. Write it as if no one else knows what you're talking about (and try to hide the fact that neither do you). There is very little point in beginning: "Sir, — If the JPC of Inverness had discussed the project with Mr Carruthers two weeks earlier, we would have had three of them by now and a much happier workforce." What's a JPC? Who is Mr Carruthers? Which project? Three of what? Which workforce? Why are they unhappy?

3. Keep it legally safe. There is a common myth that if the Press and Journal were daft enough to publish a libel, only the Editor would land in the dock. In fact, you'd be standing next to him.

4. Try to leaven it. Even the dreariest, heaviest subjects can stand wit.

5. Give us your name and full postal address, even on e-mails. You won't be published without them. Oh, and make sure it's your own name and address, not the Banchory minister's.

■ ■ ■ ■

I had hoped this would encourage readers to play the game. Alas, it didn't. We still get just as many anonymous letters, hoax letters, correspondents who don't want their names published and get quite shirty when we explain that anything less than a full postal address will make publication impossible, and correspondents who appear to think we have room for 500-word treatises.

I'm afraid the answer is still No on all counts.

22. THE NON-SPORTING LIFE

Or why physical exertion is best left to those who like it

■■■ ■■ ■■ ■■

*"I'm sorry, but I would no more join a gym than I would
go to one of those all-over tanning studios. Why scare
innocent people?"*

IT HAS been an operose week in the howe. The other night, I
returned from a day of fending off phone calls and e-mails in
the office, shook the dog's offered paw and flopped into my
usual seat at the kitchen table.

Then, in quick succession, came home-made leek-and-potato
soup, something brown and disc-shaped which tasted like, well,
something brown and disc-shaped, creamed spinach and my
favourite, mashed tatties, followed by strawberries and cream,
then coffee and a fancy piece.

I don't want to give anyone the impression that I'm anything less
than wholly delighted with this 9pm arrangement, especially
considering that Mrs Harper has put in a hard day's work herself.
I'm certainly not ungrateful or unaware that I am extremely
fortunate in the husbandly stakes. Nevertheless, I think Mrs
Harper is under the impression that I spend my working day
digging holes or running marathons. She feeds me as if there are
four much brawnier versions of me to sustain, not one writer
whose daily existence is more or less sitting at a computer screen.

This result of this full-board policy struck me the other day as I
was sitting at my desk and looked down to see that my shirt had
billowed out in much the same way as a sheet billows when the

wind catches it on the washing line. I moved to clap it back into place, except that it wouldn't clap back into place for reasons not unrelated to three-course meals late at night.

I mentioned this the other Monday when a pasta bake appeared under my nose. One doesn't like to offend the management. "There's a simple solution," she said. "You need more exercise. Take up a sport. Chocolate sauce on the ice-cream?"

Take up a sport. Have more than 40 years of avoiding wasteful and needless physical activity come to nothing? The last such close encounter, when she bought me an exercise bike, was fended off successfully as, in the process of assembly, I managed secretly to instal one component backwards, thus necessitating its return to the warehouse for a full refund.

When a gym opened in the village, she left me a few of their advertising fliers in strategic places round the house. I'm sorry, but I would no more join a gym than I would go to one of those all-over tanning studios. Why scare innocent people?

Would I consider taking up jogging? No, I would not. I hear all the propaganda about the exhilaration of the run, but consider the simple visual evidence. Every jogger you pass on the roads in the countryside, or pounding pavements in Aberdeen, looks as if he thinks his bowels are about to drop out. If it's that enjoyable, why don't its practitioners look cheerier?

Swimming, then? You must be joking. The regular cacophony of sneezing round about me in the swimming pool at secondary school put me off public dookery for life. If I want that, I can blow my nose in my bath.

Cycling? What, and be flattened by traffic?

Hillwalking? If ever I feel compelled to be swarmed by flies and midgies I can stand for a couple of hours after the dog does his business. That way, I also save on petrol.

Golf? My parents, both late converts, have been at me for years to take up this sport. It's a popular one among morning-paper journalists, mainly because a work shift that starts at lunchtime leaves an entire morning free for a round.

But it's not for me. Not only is it fiercely expensive and radioactively competitive behind the veneer of bonhomie and back-slapping, I couldn't stand the conversations about whether Titleists' trajectories favoured slow greens or whatever. The compulsion to wear violent trousers is another no-no.

Tennis? I'm sufficiently unco-ordinated that the racket which I would require to hit a ball even twice the regulation size has yet to be made. Besides, I don't like barley water.

Line dancing? Thank you, no. I know its devotees adore it, but it's basically impersonating a hen to particularly bad music.

Archery? I tried this once at school and quite liked it, which is more than could be said for the owner of the garden shed just beyond the bounds of the archery field.

Ski-ing? The best entertainment to be had from ski-ing is sitting down at the Brig on a winter Sunday morning and watching the police nabbing speeding Volvos and Audis filled with fluorescent anoraks as they head for the Lecht.

Skating, then? A sport that's free for seven days a year at most isn't going to make a dent on any waistline. Besides, the one time I tried it I couldn't stand up for long enough to find out whether or not I was any good.

Horse-riding? I've tried this. The instructor said I seemed to have a natural affinity with horses (it must be the teeth), but the saddle makes an awful mess of your jeans. Also, I don't have an estate car and the 4x4 belongs to Mrs Harper.

Angling? The requirement to embellish tales of the day's catch on your return home or in the pub would be a major obstacle. As we all know, journalists don't tell lies or exaggerate. What?

Darts? Well, I'm developing the major requirement, a straining belt, I know, but despite hours of rehearsal in front of the bedroom mirror, I can't master the po-faced stare and the pursed lips at the same time.

Table tennis? No Chinese ancestry.

Weightlifting? I do that every time I climb out of the car.

Football? I gave up this as a bad job the day I came home from primary school and told my mother that I'd had an absolutely stupendous first day on the football park and that I, and I alone, had "scored a foul".

Rugby? The Rab C. Nesbit headgear's a bit of a downer. Also, in school rugby selection the coach watched us all perform and told the boy next to me that he'd be a great full-back. He told me I'd have a great rugby career the minute anyone was looking for a draw-back.

Aerobics? The elastic went in my blue-sequin leotard just the other night. Shame.

Javelin? Discus? See Archery.

Climbing? Working in newspapers, I see quite enough stories of hillborne neepery in winter without my adding to the statistics.

Sailing? Too far from the coast.

Paragliding? Too close to the mountains.

And so on, and so on.

In the end, I suppose, it comes back to diet. I have suggested that a little less of everything would be in order, but Mrs Harper has insisted that a specialised diet will remove the surplus pounds much more quickly than would simple restraint. Consequently, she has been poring over books about the Grapefruit Diet, the F-plan Diet, the Low-Carb Diet, the High-Carb Diet and every diet known to literary agents and accountants everywhere.

I have been on the Banana Diet for several days. It's a banana mashed into milk in the mornings, a couple of bananas for lunch, a banana sandwich at teatime, followed by savoury banana mash with banana sauce, then banana ice-cream in the evenings.

It's too early to say if it works yet, but I'll let you know the minute I stop swinging on the curtain rails.

I should have foreseen that several gyms and fitness instructors throughout the North-east would contact me and offer to show me how painless it could be to get back in trim again.

I would have taken them up on their very kind offers, but I couldn't summon the energy.

23. MUFFLE THE MOANERS

Or why we're all fed up hearing other people's petty whines

▬ ▬ ▬ ▬

"Some of us appear to treat every minor darn in life's
rich tapestry as a personal slight and want compensation,
or someone punished, or both."

IT HAS been a stridulous week in the howe. You might have seen the newspaper story of the disgruntled Scottish holidaymaker who booked a trip to Ontario to see the glories of the turning leaves, only to discover when she reached the hotel that the area had suffered a particularly nasty gale a couple of days previously and that most of the leaves had not just turned, but turned tail and gone.

She wanted a refund. The hotel was equally adamant that she wasn't going to get one; that all she had booked was a room, not a treeful of scarlet and ochre leaves, and that nowhere in the brochure had the management promised a Vermont-style display.

Ayrshire's most irate matron remains undaunted and intends to raise an action in a Canadian court to get herself a refund for foliage that had vanished by the time she got there. I hope to goodness she doesn't, for she risks making herself look even more stupid than evidently she is.

We all have our disappointments. Life is full of them. We try to sail over the small ones, cope as best we can with the middling ones, and hope that the big ones are few.

Alas, some of us appear to treat every minor darn in life's rich tapestry as a personal slight and want compensation, or someone punished, or both. That's the way of modern Britain. How else can you account for the woman who wanted her ticket price refunded on a United flight because the smoked salmon tasted too fishy?

What can you say to the Leicester couple who wanted money back from a Kingussie B&B because the bathwater was peaty brown after a day of heavy rain? "Grow up" might be a good start.

Is there any hope for the doting parents of a nine-year-old who knocked out one of his front teeth by swigging too enthusiastically on a bottle of cola in an Aberdeen cafe? The parents wanted money on the grounds that the cafe should have forced the boy to use a glass.

The most entertaining are delayed holidaymakers. I can understand that delays are frustrating. I've been delayed at airports many times and it's tedious in the extreme.

But news crews and docusoap producers always manage to unearth irate Mancunian trallops sporting bad perms, bottle tans, cotton tops two sizes too small, and puffing an Embassy Regal, barking in every direction that the airline's a disgrace and that they're going to sue. Who cares, dearie? Away and have another swig of gin.

We're marginally more sanguine up here, but only just. Some of you might recall the afternoon of chaos at Aberdeen Airport early in 2001 when fog rolled in and the airport was more or less paralysed for four hours.

The Press and Journal dispatched a reporter, who returned with the news that passengers were upset at being delayed, but that almost everybody had understood that airport and airline staff were doing their best with a situation beyond their control.

I stress almost everybody, because one irate family, whose girth and concertina lirks suggested a diet that consisted of crisps, chocolate, cola, pizza and cream cakes but very little food, wanted the world to know, via the Press and Journal, that the airport's behaviour was scandalous; that staff had tried to fob them off with excuses about fog, and that they wanted a fistful of vouchers at the very least.

How I wish the Information Desk staff had handed Mummy Tub, Daddy Tub and the three teenage Tubs an electric fan each with extra long cords and suggested they went outside if they weren't happy and tried blowing away the fog on the airport's behalf.

The reflex reaction to any misadventure nowadays, however minor, is: "Compensation." If fewer people saw flashing £££ signs every time a hospital made a mistake, the National Health Service would be quids in.

No medical person wilfully makes an error, and of course the results of these errors are frequently upsetting and often tragic, yet it seems to escape the aggrieved parties that suing the NHS is actually suing all of us. It's also extending waiting lists for people who perhaps can't afford to wait.

Sometimes, you get the impression that people spend their every waking hour working hard to find offence. We're not immune at the Press and Journal. It's hard to believe, I know, but there you go. Shortly after the attacks on the World Trade Centre we took a call from a woman who complained that one of the clues in our crossword was insensitive. Dearie me.

Whenever we print a recipe for skirlie, as we do from time to time, we know to expect a call from a woman reader who feels we're being irresponsible to promote high-fat foods considering Scotland's record of heart disease. I think we're just being Scottish and certainly not quite so po-faced and joyless as the lady in question.

A couple of years ago, I answered a mid-evening call and bore an instant and irate blast from a reader who had missed a TV documentary about the D-Day landings because of an error in the TV page. I said I was sorry to hear that we'd let him down. Sorry, apparently, wasn't good enough. What did I propose to do about it? He was an old soldier. Very few programmes on TV interested him. Now he'd missed one completely thanks to newspaper incompetence.

I asked which edition he was looking at. He said he was phoning from Inverness, so I excused myself for a moment while I got a copy of that day's Inverness paper. I tried to calm him down while I flicked to Page Four, as it was in those days, to establish what the error was and why it might have arisen.

But there wasn't an error. The programme details were there in glorious black and white. The time was accurate. The title was accurate. The blurb was accurate. Even the VideoPlus number was accurate.

I suggested to him very gently that he might have made a mistake. He exploded again.

I won't trouble you with the long process of elimination that I went through with our combustible reader. Was he looking at the correct day's paper? Had he set his video recorder wrongly? Was he looking at the wrong channel?

It transpired after a couple of minutes' quizzing that he was planning his evening's viewing with a copy of The Sun.

"Hang on a minute," I said. "There's a mistake in the TV page in The Sun, but you're phoning the Press and Journal to complain?"

"I am. You're supposed to be our local paper."

You may assume that it tested all my powers of diplomacy to end that call gracefully.

Moaning and self-obsession happen in all walks of life. The day after the World Trade Centre was demolished by terrorists and 6,000 people died, a Scottish politician called the Press and Journal to acknowledge that a picture of him presenting a cheque at a Buchan function had appeared, but demanding to know why one of him gracing another Buchan function had not. This was "censorship and political bias of the worst sort".

If it was a joke, it was in very bad taste. If, as was more likely, it was rampant ego, he should have been ashamed of himself.

24. GOT THE JUMBLE-SALE BLUES

Or how to spot the bargains on a Saturday morning

━━ ━━ ━━ ━━

"Most of the men were worried that they would be ordered
to dip into their wallets for a pair of checked flares, or
Javanese wind chimes, or a home-made collage."

IT HAS been a superfluous week in the howe. Much against my better judgment, I ventured to a jumble sale at the weekend This wasn't because I am fascinated by trock or other people's unwanted Christmas presents, but because we needed to give moral support to a relative who was manning a stall and because, well, the event was for a good cause.

So, we bowled along the highways and by-ways until we reached one of the North-east's most celebrated towns.

As with most country jumbles, we found the men sitting resolutely just inside the front door of the hall, arms folded and stony-faced, worried in case they were about to be ordered to dip into their wallets for a pair of checked flares, or a set of Javanese wind chimes, or a home-made collage made from scraps of felt and marless buttons.

As strangers, we were scanned thoroughly; so thoroughly that they could scarcely have discovered any more about us had they asked us to disrobe.

Mrs Harper banked to the left to see if she could find our relative at her bric-a-brac stall. I stood in the middle of an open space, hands in my pockets, kicking my heels, knowing no one and with no one taking me on.

Much against my better judgment, I decided to saunter round the stalls. If ever you have tried to prise a double-glazing salesman from your house, or been in an Arab souk, or a Jewish jewellery shop, or any store at all in New York, you'll know what high-pressure salesmanship can be.

They're all amateurs compared to the women manning the stalls at a North-east jumble sale. You daren't say: "Just looking, thank you." They don't say anything, but the stare that follows you would set your hair on fire.

Since crocheted toilet-roll holders have never really been my bag, not even with the silk carnations on the top, I followed a crowd of brosey chiels out through a side door and found myself in a windswept yard.

For all I knew, this could have been a scam to get me outside so that I would have to pay to get in again, but I fetched up in what amounted to a jumble sale of products that had been too big or awkward or dirty to get inside the hall.

I made the mistake of stopping next to a table which seemed to be selling garden equipment, including a rather fresh-looking brushcutter. The woman behind the counter said: "Can I help ye?" She said it so sweetly that I didn't like to offer my usual: "Just looking, thank you." Instead, I said: "Is that what I think it is?" It was a pretty stupid question now that I think of it.

"Fit div ye think it is?" she said.

"I think it's a McCulloch strimmer."

She nodded. "Thirty poun," she said.

"Thirty pounds for a McCulloch strimmer?" I said. "But it looks brand new."

"Na," she said. "It's been used. I'm nae sure fit wye it's bein selt. Jimmy, fit wye's the strimmer bein selt?"

There came a bark from two stalls along. "It's bashed aboot the airm."

I looked closer and, right enough, there was a rather severe dent half-way along the aluminium shaft of the device. "So does it still work?" I said.

"I dinna ken," the woman said. "Jimmy, dis the strimmer still work?"

"No."

I looked at the woman and she looked at me. "It doesn't work at all?" I said.

"I doot no," she said. "I suppose ye could hae't for twenty-five."

"Is it repairable?" I said.

"I couldna say. Jimmy, wid the strimmer fix?"

"Dinna think so. The engine's aa richt, bit the rest o't's nae eese for nithing." As salesmen went, Jimmy wasn't exactly a master of the art.

"Bit the engine's aa richt," the stallholder said brightly as it became clear that I was going to drift away. I'm not entirely sure how I could have made use of a 38cc two-stroke engine. I could maybe have had the wheelbarrow motorised or made the dog a buggy for his old age.

Alas, no sale.

You won't be surprised to hear that I by-passed Jimmy's stall. His goods looked suspiciously dirty or faded, and many of them had had their 13-amp plugs removed, a sure sign of a nippit deal.

Two stalls beyond that, there lay a little ice-cream machine. It was a pretty simple affair: just a double-hulled bowl filled, presumably, with some sort of freezing compound, with a mixer motor at the top attached to a blade which sat inside the bowl to keep the ice-cream mixture moving while it set.

"Atween you and me," said the stallholder, whose honesty I grew to admire, "it's affa scrattit inside." I peered into the bowl and saw that its Teflon coating wasn't so much a coating as a few sorry flakes.

"So does that affect the taste of the ice-cream?"

"It means ye canna get it oot."

I peered inside the bowl again. "So if we made a batch of ice-cream, we'd have to sit round this bowl and eat it from that?"

"Or ye could let it melt."

I thanked her kindly and walked on, wondering about the worth of freezing ice-cream only to have to let it melt again to get at it, and concerned for the health of previous consumers of Vanilla-and-Teflon Ripple.

Almost every item I studied in that outdoor section of the sale turned out to be badly distressed or thoroughly extinct in some form or another, yet the stalls seemed to be doing a roaring trade.

There's obviously money in junk. Or maybe it's all recycled year after year and each item is doing its annual rounds. At least it was for charity.

I returned to the curiously pungent warmth afforded by bottled-gas portable heaters and found Mrs Harper about to join the queue for the fly-cuppery. She and I sat at the end of a trestle table and were joined by our relative, who had managed to get a 15-minute break.

The three of us discussed the success of the sale, community spirit, the superb quality of really good home baking, the fact that every sale anyone has ever attended has sold Swiss milk toffee wrapped in greaseproof paper, and has had a bottle stall comprising mainly jars of indeterminate Greek or Polish contents two weeks past their sell-by date.

And Babycham.

We were so deep in conversation that we almost missed the couple wandering past carrying their purchase proudly.

It was an ice-cream maker.

The line that still means the most to me in this column is "the curiously pungent warmth afforded by bottled-gas portable heaters".

Any rural child who has memories of being hauled along to jumble sales or bring-and-buys, or who attended public-hall Christmas parties, knows instantly which smell I mean.

I can't walk through an ironmonger's shop these days without being transported back 35 years.

25. BRITAIN BLOWS ITS STACK

Or why we're more prepared to lose our rag in public

"Just as we were certain that the musical accompaniment was over, it would start again, even louder and punctuated with whistles and rasps."

IT HAS been a bellicose week in the howe. I don't know if it's mass stress, something in the water or a phase of the moon, but the national reluctance to lose the public rag appeared to be blown apart at the weekend. At least, that's how it appeared to me. The popular notion that the British are reserved and unhappy to stand up for themselves, meaning that they have to endure all manner of nonsense, has been a feature of the national character for years.

Mrs Harper still reminds me of the time in a Glasgow restaurant when the food was distinctly below par: cold, overcooked and with a faint hint that it had been reheated from frozen.

The cutlery had streaks. The glasses had scratches that spoke of several years of hard use, and when the carpet had last seen a vacuum cleaner wasn't entirely clear. Neither was the evening particularly cheap.

So I fulminated, muttered and grumbled all through the first and main courses, as men do, resolving in a stage whisper that the whole place was a rip-off of astronomical proportions; it was no surprise that the tourist industry was in a slump; there had better not be service charge on the bill; the complaints form would be red hot, and we would never darken their door again.

Then a waitress appeared at my right shoulder and said in her bright, cheery Glaswegian way: "Is everything all right?" And I heard myself say: "Yes, fine, thank you."

Mrs Harper has never let me live it down.

Even with good cause, the British have an inhibition about really letting rip in public. We fume and stew while on holiday abroad about poor food or constant noise or the mould on the bathroom tiling, but we wait until we get home, then write a letter of complaint to the tour company.

Well, not any more. I was on a flight to London at the weekend, and squeezed into my seat past an ample chap in his late 40s. I say ample, but huge would be nearer the mark. His prominent tum and bull thighs presented quite an obstacle, so I more fell into my seat than sat in it.

He had the tanned complexion of someone who had been on a prolonged holiday, and the T-shirt and shorts ensemble completed the effect. If I tell you that he had the look of a rugby-playing police inspector on extended leave, you get the picture.

Within minutes of the plane taking off, he was asleep. Within minutes of drifting off, his jaw dropped and the snoring began.

It was amusing enough at the start. The man across the aisle would look up from his magazine, study the snorer, catch my eye and grin. Every so often, the snorer would catch his breath, cough and splutter, but never awaken. Then a few seconds of blissful silence would follow. Just as we were certain that the musical accompaniment was over, it would start again, even louder and punctuated with whistles and rasps.

I've heard quite a few snorers in my time, but this man was an orchestra of pneumatic drills. With every roar, my meal tray, and those of several passengers round about, was vibrating across the seatback table.

As interest spread throughout the cabin, passengers four rows forwards and backwards from us were sitting up in their seats to see if a bull walrus had boarded, unbeknownst to the crew. It is difficult in these circumstances to try to convey to strangers who are scowling and frowning, or laughing and smiling, that the snorer has nothing to do with you.

By the time the snoring had gone beyond the point of being funny, I began making a pretence of dropping things, hoping that the noise would wake him up. I was forgetting completely, of course, that we were sitting aboard a passenger jet, atop two RB211 engines going a full pelt. If he was sleeping through that, he was unlikely to be stirred by a dropped Biro.

The man across the aisle began clapping his hands sharply, to no avail. The cabin crew turned up the volume on the cabin announcements. No success.

And then it happened. A little woman in the seat directly in front of him sat bolt upright and turned round. "You," she said, and the snorer spluttered and blinked awake. "You. Are you getting medical attention for that awful racket?"

He blinked once or twice while he came to himself, then peered round slowly at the sea of expectant faces throughout the cabin. "I didna sleep aa last nicht," he said.

"That's immaterial," said the woman, whom I thought considerably feisty, since she was as slight as he was bullnecked, and he might easily have flung her several rows forward with little more than a flick of his wrist.

"That makes no difference to any of these poor people round about you. You have ruined everyone's very expensive journey with your selfishness. Get medical attention. That was disgusting."

And she sat down again, disappearing into the bulk of her seat. The funniest of the exchange was that for the short time that remained, the snorer sat bolt upright, staring straight ahead and gripping the seat arms, evidently terrified of falling asleep again.

Once off the plane, I went to the Left Luggage counter to leave my bags for a few hours before I checked in for a later flight.

To say that the service was tortoise-slow would have been an insult to reptiles. In front of me for more than 45 minutes stood the same six customers, while the three teenagers who were meant to be in charge of the place shambled and mooched about behind the counter, unperturbed about achieving much of anything.

They would shuffle paperwork, riffle through the till, blink slowly as if mesmerised by 21st-century existence, then shamble across to the other side of the counter for some more shuffling and mumbling. I was getting a little agitated myself with this performance when a distinguished-looking 50-ish gentleman in front of me finally blew. "Get me the manager," he said. The three teenagers looked up as one: Dopey, Ropey and Mopey.

"Get me the manager," said the man again. "This is disgraceful."

"Ya go"a be patient," said the lead sloth.

That heaved on more petrol. "Patient? Be patient? I've been standing here for very nearly an hour, for a very expensive service, and you're telling me to be patient? This is precisely the sort of thing which gets the United Kingdom a very bad name with visitors." Three American-looking souls up front began nodding approval. "We been waitin more'n an hour," said one. "Ah think Ah've taken root."

"We want some service." said the Englishman.

"Ya ge"in service," said the teenager in that most unappealing Estuary English.

"Service? As what? Cabaret? The monkeys' tea party? The dunces' class?"

The Americans stepped forward, emboldened by the vigour of the Englishman's complaint, and began stabbing fingers at the beleaguered staff. The teenagers just blinked and looked even dopier as the League of Nations onslaught gathered momentum.

I, meanwhile, picked up my bags and left. Being lumbered with my chattels for four hours, I decided, would be a small price to pay for escaping a minor riot.

——— ——— ——— ———

I didn't mention in this column that the little woman who berated the snorer let slip that she was a doctor.

If even a medical professional could get so irritated, perhaps that gives you an inkling as to how bad the snoring really was.

26. HEAT OF THE MOMENT

Or why a spell of sunshine has curious effects

▬ ▬ ▬ ▬

"He said he felt extremely comfortable at this point;
unabashed by his nudity because everyone else was
unabashed by theirs."

IT HAS been a sudorific week in the howe. Like most of the
country, you'll have been enjoying the scorching weather
these past few days. Already, the North and North-east are
symphonies of tomato noses, lobster arms and softly moaning
queues at the chemist for calamine lotion.

Not that I'm wishing away the fine weather, you understand, but
we dream of it for 48 weeks of the year and then lose the place
completely when it arrives.

Doctors will tell you of their surgeries being stuffed to bursting
with screaming babies because the parents hadn't the wit to offer
the wee ones some shade.

Pharmacists will tell you of customers whose skin is peeling so
badly that they look as if they are climbing out of a very large and
very tattery polythene bag.

Policemen will tell you that heat brings mass hysteria to the
public, when otherwise civil people will blow a gasket at the
slightest provocation. In other words, be extra careful when it's
hot. People do the daftest things.

On a trip to Edinburgh during that first hot spell at the end of
April, Mrs Harper and I parked the car outside the Royal Botanical
Garden West Gate. There was enough heat in the air for me to

know that we would be returning to a four-wheeled furnace shortly after lunchtime, so I did what every car-security expert says you should never do: I left the windows open half an inch.

I did it only after Mrs Harper had begun walking away because I didn't want my Sunday stroll round the Botanic spoiled with a constant lecture about thieves, footpads and returning to an empty space in the street. So we spent five hours ambling round the garden as the capital roasted gently.

By 2pm, visitors were flaking out on the grass in the shade of whichever trees they could find, and we opted to head back for the car and the drive north. It was still there, so we let the doors stand open for a minute to let out the worst of the heat, then climbed in, belted up, and I started the engine.

Remembering that I had left the windows open slightly, and hoping to keep my deliberate foolishness a secret, I stabbed at the window buttons to shut them. Alas, just as I stabbed the button, Mrs Harper lifted her finger to feel the gap and said: "Look at this. My window seems to be opeNNNNNN."

I got such a shock that I looked up to see what had gone wrong. She was hanging there, like a blonde primate dangling one-handed from its climbing frame, her finger jammed tightly between the window glass and the top of the door, and screaming blue murder.

My mind went blank. I couldn't find the switch again for fully five seconds, but then I was able to free her.

Three weeks later, her forefinger is still numb and I still want to know what happened to the safety cutout of the window mechanism. I also want to know if any other grown woman pokes her fingers into unexpected apertures. What next? Shoving her digits into mains sockets? Ramming dried peas in her ears?

You have to look after them all the time.

This mesmerising effect of heat strikes the best of us. One of Mrs Harper's teaching colleagues took a notion during a hot spell several years ago to do some work on the outside of his house. Men are like that. He set the ladder beside the first-floor window, climbed up and set about whatever he had to do.

Work had been going well for about an hour or so until he

decided either that he needed something from inside the house, or something cold to drink, or whatever. So he stepped to the left.

Stepping to left isn't entirely sensible when you're 15ft up a ladder. The resulting dental work needed a small mortgage.

In the blistering heatwave in April, 1998, my aunt decided to go for a paddle in the sea a short distance from her holiday hotel. As I watched from the safety of the pier, she bundled her handbag under her oxter, lifted her skirt a little higher and stepped into the water. She got herself accustomed for a few moments then, emboldened, she ventured farther.

And farther.

The calm waters had seduced her, but she hadn't noticed that a real surfer's wave was forming 50 yards out to sea. Alas, 4ft6in wifies and 8ft waves don't mix very well. Other people on the pier began shouting warnings. She looked up at them, then out to sea, panicked, turned, and started doing her best to wade the 15 yards back to shore. That's not easy when you're 4ft6in and 70 and carrying a handbag the size of a small suitcase.

With half the people on the pier firing up their camcorders, my aunt did her best, but eventually the wave caught her, knocked her to her knees and submerged her.

People on the shoreline waded in, lifted her up quickly and beached her. There she lay, a drookit rat, but Scottish to the last: her handbag was still rammed under her oxter. Her only complaint was that her bag of fizzy sweeties had fizzed beyond repair.

Younger people are affected by heat hysteria, too. Several years ago, a gang of our tele-ads staff went on a girls' holiday to the hotspots of Spain. Being Aberdonians, they were less than keen to follow the topless example of German and Dutch women on all sides of them.

Eventually, and with a lot of mutual daring, they reasoned that there was nothing to embarrass them. It wasn't as if anyone they knew would see them. So they removed their bikini tops.

While they were still rubbing in suntan oil, they heard: "Aye-aye, quines. Rare day." Strolling past was a Press and Journal van driver, also on holiday.

My favourite sun story, though, comes from the AA. During the heatwave of 1976, they received a plea to attend a breakdown at a holiday camp on the English South Coast.

The patrolman was stopped at the gate and told that he could go no farther.

Why? It was a nudist colony. The patrolman was told he could enter, but not clothed.

Showing dedication far beyond the call, he agreed to drive to a small block near the entrance and strip off. He appeared, looking extremely white compared to everybody else, with his little bag of spanners and was taken to the place where the sick car lay in beating sunshine.

He said he felt surprisingly comfortable at this point; unabashed by his nudity because everyone else was unabashed by theirs. By the time he met the owner of the stricken car, he was beginning to understand the appeal of holidays in the buff.

When the car-owner told him that the problem was a grinding noise from under the bonnet, the patrolman lifted the hood, stuck the bonnet prop in place . . . and then made his big mistake. He leaned over to peer into the engine.

Car bodywork gets extremely hot when it has been lying in 85F sunshine for a whole day.

He had to be taken to hospital for a serious and embarrassing contact burn. There were no volunteers to apply calamine lotion.

■■ ■■ ■■ ■■

Occasionally, a column results in a letter from a younger reader, and this was one such column.

A primary-school pupil from Peterhead way wrote to ask if I had heard about the Fraserburgh man who had suffered very bad sunburn. The doctor had examined him and said it was his own fault.

Apparently, he'd been basking for it.

27. WHATEVER HAPPENED TO CHARACTERS?

Or why community worthies haven't really disappeared

━━ ━━ ━━ ━━

*"They were just the fixtures and fittings of our villages or
towns; the people whose devil-may-care ways occasioned
much gossip and hilarity at least once a week."*

IT HAS been a tralineate week in the howe. One of the
clarions of modern Scottish society, particularly from people
of, shall we say, a more mature vintage, is that there aren't the
characters about nowadays that there used to be.

It's always said with a degree of regret, even sadness; as if
today's monotonous, nine-to-five, homogeneous lot pales by
comparison with the glorious eccentrics of old. If you've caught
yourself saying or thinking something along these lines, you're in
the majority. I don't know many people who don't hold similar
views.

However old we are, we look back on some of the colourful
and pungent rogues of our youth, either by acquaintance or
reputation, and wonder where the modern equivalents might be.

You could be thinking of people such as Sawdust Calder, who
used to tramp the bars of Aberdeen selling sawdust for scattering
on the floors. You might be thinking of Benedetto Suave, whose
great, characterful face was such a feature of between-the-wars
Aberdeen, when he was northern Scotland's only professional
organ-grinder. No word on the monkey.

Some of the more daring of you might have memories of Snuffy
Ivy or Cove Mary, whose activities I can't explore here.

119

I can think of several classic characters from my own boyhood, as can most people in the howe. Indeed, every parish, hamlet, village town and city had them. My contention today is that everywhere still has them. We just don't realise it.

We don't realise it in much the same way that none of us realised that the characters of our youth were characters. They were just the fixtures and fittings of our villages or towns; the people whose devil-may-care ways occasioned much gossip and hilarity at least once a week. They didn't become "characters" until we had lost them and it was too late to appreciate them for the free spirits they had been.

I did a straw poll of my colleagues to hear tales of their own childhoods and youth. If some of you share home towns with these people, you'll recognise the rogues I'm about to describe.

You'll recognise the bachelor farmhand who was fond of a drappie now and again, but who could never stop at just the one. He was good with his hands, so he made up an elaborate form of the egg-crate, pram-wheels cartie that most of us had in our schooldays. This one was built with a harness at the front, shaped and fitted ideally for the man's trusty collie.

At closing time, your man would stumble from the hostelry, fold himself into the cartie in whatever haphazard manner he could manage, all legs and elbows, and call: "Home."

The dog would then nose into the harness and haul its master the half-mile back to their cottar hoosie.

You might think that was a well-trained dog, although my colleague says that it seemed to pass without much remark in the village, probably because it was so commonplace. We are notoriously hard to impress in North and North-east Scotland. Now, if the dog had been trained to remove its master's dungars and put him to bed . . .

One Banffshire town was home in the 1960s to a couple who seemed like candidates for an early divorce. It appeared that almost every time they ventured out in public together, an almighty spat ensued, using the sort of language that you and I don't know exists.

They might have been having a fly cup in a café or a quiet drink in one of the town bars and one would begin needling the other. The needle would become a shouting match. The shouting would look as if it might come to blows. Invariably, the café manageress or the bar manager would invite them to leave.

The curious thing was that they were affectionate and attentive in the bounds of their own home, and their visitors couldn't believe the contrast between the couple's private and public behaviour.

Popular rumour held that the public arguments were the duo's ploy to get out of paying for their stovies, or their buttery and syrup, or standing their hand. If that was the case, it certainly worked. Repeatedly.

There was Jimmy, the inhabitant of one Garioch village from the 1940s to the 1970s. Had anyone thought to hold a Worst Driver in History competition, Jimmy would have won the gold medal and a bottle of champagne. That man went through more gearboxes than Michael Schumacher.

Jimmy came from an era when driving tests hadn't been invented and, my goodness, it showed. His attitude to parking was that since other cars had steering wheels, they could manoeuvre round about him, no matter where he chose to abandon his vehicle, usually several feet from the pavement.

His attitude to signalling was equally debonair. Frequently, a symphony of screeching brakes and tooting horns would rent the Garioch air as Jimmy trundled off to right or left without advance warning. As he would explain later: "The boy should hiv kent I aye turn that wye."

Jimmy's car was the only one in the whole of the Garioch that bore curious streaks along the paintwork on both flanks. These were scrapes occasioned by the fact that Jimmy managed a clean entry of his garage about one time in three. The dull front bumpers spoke of the times he hadn't quite managed to tap the brakes before the car tapped the garage's back wall.

There are dozens more characters. There's the man who dressed up as a woman one Friday night to make a hasty escape from police officers on his trail. It can't have worked very well, for it has passed into the folklore of one Aberdeenshire village.

There was the middle-aged professional man of a vengeful turn of mind who made a habit of taking out his spite on people he imagined had crossed him by unscrewing the petrol caps on their cars when they weren't around and quietly urinating into their fuel tanks.

My source tells me that since most of the slights were in the phantom urinator's imagination only, his victims had no inkling that they had offended him until their cars sputtered to a halt. You'll all be pleased that fuel caps are lockable these days.

In Aberdeen, there was Tattie Meg, whose monicker came not from the humble root vegetable, but from her habit of wearing hosiery that had long since seen better days. The multiple apertures in the nylon allowed her bare flesh to swell through in various places, making it seem for all the world that two columns of potatoes were walking up the street.

Where are the modern equivalents of all these people? Trust me, they're about. They're not far off, either. Every village and town throughout northern Scotland is entertained and bemused by their antics on a regular basis.

You know who they are perfectly well.

We just don't appreciate them yet.

We got a smashing letter from a woman at Cults not long after this column appeared. Her family had known and spoken regularly to Benedetto Suave, the organ-grinder, during World War II.

Apparently, Signor Suave was a staunch supporter of the British war effort, despite his Italian background. He would opine: "King George, good. Churchill, good. Roosevelt, good. Mussolini, nae bliddy eese ata."

28. ALISTAIR, A MAN WITH STYLE

Or why seemingly detached people perhaps have it right after all

▬▬ ▬▬ ▬▬ ▬▬

"Alistair won't mind me saying this, but he is forgetful.
Detached. Divorced from the world which the rest of us
inhabit. A daydreamer."

IT HAS been an amnemonic week in the howe. There I was, sitting at my desk, working my way through something or other, when the phone rang. That's not an unusual occurrence in a newspaper office, you understand. The tyranny of ringing phones is more pronounced here than anywhere else I can imagine short of a call centre.

This call turned out to be different. This was a voice from my past.

It was a call from a former colleague I hadn't seen or spoken to since he retired in the late 1980s and moved back to his home airt in the Glasgow area. We'll call him Alistair, rather than using his real name, for reasons which will become apparent. We all liked him too much for me now to draw public attention to his many eccentricities.

Alistair had felt like a chat, so he had lifted the phone in his home in the Central Belt and had called me. You have to know Alistair to understand that the gap of 11 years had simply not happened as far as he was concerned. The tone of his call was almost as if he was phoning in on the last evening of a fortnight's holiday to check what shift he had been assigned for the following week.

123

Alistair won't mind me saying this, because he has admitted as much to me and most of my colleagues on many occasions since first we got to know him. Alistair is forgetful. Detached. Divorced from the world which the rest of us inhabit. A daydreamer.

I always imagined that when Alistair had been in his teens, twenties and thirties, hordes of women had wanted to mother him. Probably some of the stranger ones wanted to mother him in his fifties and sixties, too. I don't doubt that there are still a few of that mind now that he is in his seventies.

He had that lost look; the air of a man who existed in a dimension untouched by mortal cares, which sometimes made the many strangers he met in the course of his journalistic work wonder if he was feeling entirely 100%. One or two called me after meeting him to hope that he would be feeling better soon.

I liked Alistair, because he was the only man who made me look organised.

He was forgetful. It was an unwritten rule at Aberdeen Journals throughout the 1980s that if spectacles were found anywhere on the premises, they were to be taken first to Alistair's desk because he would be the likeliest owner.

This rule applied no matter how unlikely the spectacles looked or however unusual their location. Alistair and his wife frequently had guests to stay and Alistair was sufficiently absent-minded to leave the house taking someone else's glasses instead of his own.

This explained several days in the office throughout his career when he sported surprisingly feminine looking specs. Whether or not he could see with them, we never liked to ask.

He was accident-prone. A colleague remembers Alistair's look of despair when he broke his favourite tea mug. Too dedicated to leave his post to buy a new one, he rooted around in an office cupboard and came out, triumphant, with a dusty crystal tumbler that must have been used last to toast someone's health in 1971, judging by the look of it. For several days after that, Alistair drank his tea from a crystal tumbler, earning himself salutes from the men and a curtsey or two from the women; honours which Alistair accepted with his customary self-effacement.

We waited several times for the loud crack of near-boiling water meeting cut glass, but it never happened. Alistair led that sort of charmed life.

You had to work hard to keep up with Alistair in a conversation, mainly because he had been pondering the topic of his choice for several minutes before he actually engaged you in the chat. He would wade straight in, seeming to believe that you had been privy to his thoughts for the previous five minutes.

Thus, it was a bit like switching on the radio and trying to pick up the threads of an obscure drama.

A typical conversation would start something like:

"So it turned out to be blue after all."

You would offer some anodyne response, hoping that the next line would fill in some of the detail. Perhaps:

"Is that so? That must have been a bit of a surprise."

"Well, the boy said that was all they had left, although they could have delivered within a couple of days if they'd known him."

"I see. Why did they need to know him?"

"Well, a company doesn't just hand over something that price without knowing you; not unless the sales people do their checks first."

And so on, and so on until, five minutes of treading conversational water later, you would work out between sentences that Alistair's son had tried to order a silver car from a Rover dealership, but had been told that the delivery delay on a silver car would be three weeks. That delay could have been cut to a couple of days, however, for a favoured, regular customer whose credit was good, and provided another Scottish dealer had the required vehicle in stock. However, the dealership had a blue car in stock and if Alistair's son compromised on colour, he could take it away there and then.

All of Alistair's conversations were like that. He certainly kept your wits sharp.

But my favourite Alistair story concerns a phone call I got one morning before I had even taken off my coat and sat at my desk. It was the stationmaster of the town from which Alistair commuted every day of his working life at the Press and Journal.

"Is that Norman Harper?"

"Yes."

"Do you know someone called Alistair?"

"I do. What's happened?"

"Nothing to worry about. It's the stationmaster at xxxxx here. Alistair was boarding his train as usual this morning and it started moving off before he realised it was going in the wrong direction. He boarded the Up train by mistake instead of the Down one. He opened a window and shouted at me on the platform to phone and let you know that, at the moment, he seems to be heading in the general direction of Inverness. He'll try not to be long, assuming he can find a train heading the right way."

Many of the older hands at the Press and Journal have dined out on that story for the last 15 years, including Alistair himself.

It was all the more puzzling, as he admitted himself, given that he would have had to put work into making the mistake. He'd have had to cross the line by footbridge to board the Inverness-bound train at the opposite platform. Who knows what was occupying his mind as he did so.

But that was the glory of Alistair. You never knew what was coming next.

━━ ━━ ━━ ━━

Someone sent a cutting of this column to Alistair at his new abode in Strathclyde. I'm delighted to say that he hadn't taken offence at all and that he and his family had recognised many and various truths about him.

He phoned again afterwards, and just as I was thinking that he had changed completely from the Alistair I once knew, he called me Ron.

29. WRONG ARM OF THE LAW

Or why the compulsion to sue is taking over

"That's the sort of madness that overtakes a country in
which everyone knows his rights, but a diminishing
number will shoulder responsibilities that go with them."

IT HAS been a clamant week in the howe. If you have been reading the papers as closely as I, you must have been marvelling at the human capacity for trying to make a buck. I'm thinking specifically of Jimmy Håkansson, a prisoner in Sweden, who is taking legal action against Stockholm Police this week.

Jimmy had been taken from the cells to the Stockholm courthouse to appear on a preliminary charge of receiving stolen goods. Two policemen had shown him to an interview room where his lawyer had been waiting to discuss his plea with him. The bobbies had withdrawn to stand outside the door.

In the middle of his little legal chat, Jimmy had leaped up from the table, raced over to the window, flung it open and jumped out. It was just a pity that the interview room was on the third floor. Jimmy broke his right foot in the fall and sprained his back so badly that he will be lying on boards for at least a month.

Now here's the good bit: Jimmy feels that Stockholm Police should have done more to stop him escaping. Not guarding him while he was speaking to his lawyer was a dereliction of police duty, he feels, so he will sue for compensation for being looked after so badly.

It has a certain style to it, don't you think? Given the example that Jimmy has set, who knows where this might end. You might soon be hearing of smokers who want to sue tobacco companies; football fans blaming breweries and pubs for the violence at 6pm games, or housebreakers trying to prosecute victims who have the effrontery to smack them in the mouth or shoot them.

This curious grasp on what's right and what's wrong appears to have started, like so many other current Western trends, in the United States, where rapacious lawyers have made a killing out of whamming up the most trivial incidents into multimillion-dollar lawsuits.

There was the famous case of the woman who tried suing McDonalds for $1million because she had burned her mouth on coffee in a paper cup. She argued that the coffee cup should have had a message printed on it to warn that fresh coffee was hot.

A woman from Denver wanted to sue Procter and Gamble because her husband had drunk bleach. Yes, bleach. Why any grown man in his right mind would want a swig of Parozone, I'm not sure, but there you go. P&G pointed out, not unreasonably, that the bottle had a safety top and that it would have been impossible to open the bottle and drink accidentally.

The woman's legal team retorted that the safety top was intended to protect children, not adults, and that for the benefit of grown-ups the bottle should have carried a large-print message reading:

Do Not Drink

A drunk who staggered down an embankment and on to the I-5 freeway through Greater Los Angeles was promptly flattened by passing traffic. He wanted to sue General Motors because the can which had hit him and had broken both his legs had had bumpers which did not deform on impact to lessen damage to pedestrians.

A printing firm in Pittsburgh had to defend itself against an action by one of its new members of staff in 1982. The apprentice complained that constant close proximity to ink made him dirty and that he had to have a shower and wash his work clothes every day. This was costing him much more than he thought was proper, and his supervisor had laughed at him when he had complained. He decided to use the law to teach the company a lesson. His case was thrown out.

Starbucks Coffee, the Seattle chain that is spreading its tentacles worldwide, must now regret selling a domestic coffee percolator from one of its shops to a particular California customer.

The machine didn't work as well as the customer had hoped, so he took it back and asked for a refund. Starbucks said no, because a company representative saw signs that the customer had abused the machine and that this was why it wasn't working. The customer then asked for a replacement machine. Again, Starbucks said: "No."

So the customer took the chain to court. As you might expect, Starbucks defended vigorously. After more than two years of court work, the judge awarded the case to the customer. Starbucks, and most of the legal and retail fraternities, was astonished.

The company was even more astonished when the judge asked the customer what he wanted as compensation. The victor said he wanted a new coffee machine, plus a new community centre for the underprivileged youngsters in his neighbourhood.

Starbucks was of a mind to appeal, but its PR consultancy advised board members to swallow their pride, pay up and look cheerful rather than look mean in the media. The case cost Starbucks more than $4.6million, and all because a $69 percolator didn't work the way one customer thought it should.

This madness has crossed the Atlantic, of course. Soon, Britons will have no need to start litigation in the US in the hope of higher compensation awards. They'll be able to do it perfectly well in the UK.

We've already had the £1,000 tea stain on a bedsheet, and the prisoner who felt aggrieved that the prison laundry had made such a bad job of his designer civvies.

We had the disgraceful case in early 1998 of the young driver of a BMW who hit and, if I remember correctly, killed a small boy who had run out in front of him. The driver stopped, but only to rant at the dying boy and his parents: "Look what you've done to my car!"

That's the sort of madness that overtakes a country in which everyone knows his rights, but a diminishing number will shoulder the responsibilities that go with them.

I'm wondering now if there will soon be a suit filed by a Welsh tourist against a South African bus operator.

The 21-year-old engineering student and a horde of his mates were returning from a rugby tour of the country and, specifically, from a day-off trip to Stellenbosch, heart of the South African vineyards, north-west of Cape Town.

As students are liable to do, especially after a vineyard crawl, your man thought it would be great fun to drop his trousers and pants and press his bare behind against the back window of the bus to shock and scare following motorists.

Alas, the window was not fixed, as is required in law of UK coaches. This window was hinged at the top and loose at the bottom to make an emergency exit easier.

At first press of posterior to glass, the window did what it was designed to do and tilted open. He fell backwards and dropped on to the middle lane of the motorway at more than 70mph.

Whatever tattery bits are left of his behind are now bandaged in a Cape Town hospital.

━━ ━━ ━━ ━━

The deliberate needle in this one, of course, was that the accusation that we'd soon be seeing smokers suing tobacco companies, football fans blaming breweries for football-match drunkenness and housebreakers wanting to sue householders who fought back had all just happened at the time that the column appeared.

The football fans, especially, didn't like it.

30. SCARES OF A SCOTTISH UPBRINGING

Or why inspiring fear plays such an effective role in child-rearing

■■ ■■ ■■ ■■

"Distress parenting is highly effective and super efficient,
but it doesn't half burden a child with a lifetime of
irrational fears and phobias."

I T HAS been a numinous week in the howe. For some reason, I appear to have had a little more time to myself in the mornings of late. Not much, just a little. I wish I could say I have been using it to do something constructive but, frankly, I'm at the stage where I need a little slobbing around, which is why I have spent the last few days mesmerised by morning television.

If morning TV is your bag, good luck to you, but I've rarely seen so little material whammed up and stretched out to fill so much air time. Those of you who still harbour the notion that British TV is the best in the world should try Kilroy or Trisha one morning.

Gape as egomaniacs with bad perms shout each other down, or the terminally depressed bare their souls and fumble for Kleenex. These people are apparently too traumatised and self-conscious to speak to their families, the people who are best placed to help them, but they can blast their woes nationwide no bother at all to millions who couldn't care less.

It's a curious country, right enough.

Recently, one Kilroy programme explored the anguish of couples who couldn't have children. I don't demean the problem. Life must seem desperate to people who live every waking second longing to have family, but after 40 minutes in which every third sentence began with: "I want . . . I want . . . We want . . ." in a Cockney whine, I had to switch off.

I want my own private helicopter, an island in the South Pacific and a lifetime supply of chocolate digestives, but nobody guaranteed that I would get them, and I wouldn't go on national TV to wail that the system had refused to provide.

It's not a statutory right, put it that way.

I accepted long ago that I would never become a dad. Not for me the adoring gaze of my eight-year-old son as I bash my thumb into the kitchen wall with a claw hammer. Not for me the glow of pride while sitting in the audience at the school panto. Not for me the pit of anxiety as my teenage daughter goes off on her first proper date.

If I need the company of small children, I can always hire my nephews for a few hours and that will do nicely. I doubt that I could have sired and raised two to match them.

Besides, not fathering anything is a major contribution to modern Scotland. It helps to stop in its tracks the phenomenon that has been the scourge of centuries: parenting by distress.

You might not be familiar with the term, but if you were born and raised in these parts you'll be aware of the practice. You'll certainly be aware of the results, for these will be with you to the grave.

Parenting by distress — I believe some psychologists call it auto-discipline — involves instilling such a basic fear in the child that he daren't misbehave or grow too bold.

You know the sort of thing. "Don't go out on the main road; people stop their cars and take you away to Africa." "Don't touch the bottles under the sink; some of them explode in your face if they're moved too quickly." "Always clean your teeth last thing at night; because insects come in the dark sniffing for dirty ones and they pull them out while you're sleeping."

It certainly did the business. Kidnappers had no prospects with me. I would never have been rushed to hospital after swigging Jeyes Fluid. I had the cleanest teeth (and bloodiest gums) in the whole of the howe.

One the other hand, I didn't go anywhere; I sat on the end of my bed from morning to night, and I was 26 before I could summon the courage to strike a match.

That's the thing about distress parenting: it's highly effective and super-efficient, but it doesn't half burden a child with a lifetime of irrational fears and phobias. For many years, I thought these applied only to me, but I discovered later, in conversation with contemporaries, that distress parenting was standard practice throughout northern Scotland.

One man believed throughout his childhood that every 100th person to pull the arm on a fruit machine got an electric shock. It was a mean thing for his parents to suggest, but it saved him a fortune in pocket money.

One woman of 45 that I know still can't walk any closer than 20ft in front of parked lorries because she had been told as a child that they sometimes jumped their transmissions, lurched forward five or six feet and caused horrible deaths.

One of my colleagues from my training days has raced motorbikes, abseiled down sheer cliff faces, gone paragliding in the Mediterranean and jumped out of planes at 15,000ft.

But he can't screw up the courage to fill a paraffin heater.

Even history was turned to a purpose in our house. When some world-shattering event was being broadcast late in the evening on TV, my father would haul me out of bed, sit me down on the sofa and tell me that I was witnessing history and that I would remember it for life.

On that basis, I remember Kennedy's funeral. I saw Churchill's gun carriage trundle through the streets of London in 1965. I saw Francis Chichester sailing into port after his round-the-world voyage.

But I was also hauled up one night to look at a documentary which seemed to consist of people in white coats poking sticks at a pile of black jelly.

These were human lungs turned to pulp by a lifetime of smoking. I was instructed to watch, then, when the programme was finished, was warned that that was what happened to little boys' insides if they so much as touched a cigarette packet. Then I was sent back to bed and wished sweet dreams.

People of my vintage, of course, suffered double assault. Not only did our parents scare the stuffing out of us, public-information films on television backed them up. Hands up who remembers the hooded ghost of still waters, hovering like death over stagnant ponds and waiting to lure careless children to a watery end?

What about the little boy who played with matches in his bedroom while everyone else was out of the house? Remember? He set fire to his bedspread. The closing shot, in which his tearful little face glowed with reflected flames and, trapped in a bedroom corner, he shouted: "Muuuum!" brings thousands of 40-year-olds out in a sweat even now.

Most effective of all, though, were the tooth-decay demons, who waited until children popped a last-minute sweet from the bedside jar into their mouths, paused to let the children fall asleep, then took out an array of picks to spend the whole night demolishing healthy teeth.

All things considered, it's a wonder that we turned out as well-adjusted and sane as we are.

Pass me my ballet tights and frogman's flippers.

Other public-information films that sprang to mind at the time were the warnings not to run round corners in case you bumped into things; the little girl running down a slope in a public park, tripping and gashing her knee on a broken bottle, and the hedgehog that had a hard time crossing the road because of roaring traffic.

Sometimes, you wonder why the Government spent the money to make them.

31. WHAT'S IN A NAME?

Or why parents should be careful before lumbering their children

▬ ▬ ▬ ▬

"Be careful how you name your offspring because it will colour the child's whole life; how people perceive and treat him or her as a youngster, adult or pensioner."

IT has been an yclept week in the howe. You'll have seen the coverage in some of the Sunday supplements and on one or two of those morning-magazine TV shows, all devoted to the latest research from academia.

The findings seemed remarkably similar to other such psychology projects at various intervals over the past 20 years, but this one was a co-production between Manchester University and Stanford in the US, so it must be good.

It's long and involved, but it boils down to one simple fact to which all imminent parents should pay heed: be careful how you name your offspring, because it will colour the child's whole life. From cradle to grave, that one decision of yours will shape how other people perceive and treat him or her as a youngster, adult and pensioner.

It will influence the degree of encouragement the child will receive from others; how people will support and favour it, and certainly will be a factor in how eager people will be to despise it and even impede it in all its life's ambitions.

Although the report's authors admitted that they could not find enough evidence to render their theory rock-solid, their confidence stemmed mainly from analysing exam results in 23 universities and almost 200 high schools on either side of the Atlantic, and seeing signs that pupils burdened with naffer names were scoring more poorly.

They conceded that they could not attribute that directly to teachers and lecturers despising naff names. Neither could they say that distaste for naff names led to examiners marking harder or teachers shunning naffly named students in myriad subtle ways.

It could have been, equally, they suggested, that pupils saddled with a dull monicker lacked confidence because of their daily uphill burden. The research team simply didn't know.

Which was all very well, but nowhere in the coverage that I saw in the newspapers and on the wire services was there any definition of what constituted a naff name. Who decides what is naff and what isn't? More important, I found no guidance for parents-to-be on what names to avoid.

So here's my tip. I can't claim copyright because I have a vague memory of reading it in an otherwise dull novel 15 or 20 years ago. It is simply this: if you can't imagine a British king or queen with the name in question, that name is very likely naff.

It might be naff at this very minute. It might be naff for various short periods of the individual's life as the name goes in and out of fashion on a regular cycle.

Alternatively, for the extremely unfortunate (Normans, for instance), it will be naff throughout the poor blighter's existence.

I hate my first name. I hated it when I was small. I hate it now. I suspect I will roll past the blue curtains at the crematorium still hating it.

It has sunk to such depths in the vast panoply of naffness that a sweetie manufacturer uses it to get a cheap laugh for a chocolate bar in TV advertisements. I have stopped eating Twixes as a matter of principle. Bad enough that they make fun of the name, but they dress the actor in a bobble hat, an anorak, jam-jar glasses and give him goofy teeth.

That, to the nation, is what it means to be a Norman. How can anyone's street cred survive that?

Whenever a TV comedy wants to introduce a two-dimensional butt for the lead characters' sharp one-liners, he's called Norman.

Norman is TV shorthand for slow wit, poor taste and general gawpitness. What do you mean, the case rests?

When I call companies Down South and have to leave my name, I can hear whoever is on the other end of the line repeating the name out loud for no good reason apart from turning to their nearest colleagues and smirking.

When I meet someone who previously was only a voice on the phone, the person pauses and says: "But I was expecting you to be about 60."

I attended a wedding reception in the Home Counties in 1980 and squirmed as all the young blades on the groom's side made me the centre of ridicule for fully five minutes until I did what I should have done four minutes sooner and managed to squeeze out a pained and strangled laugh of my own and walked away.

Even in the arms of my beloved, I am not safe. We were sitting watching TV one Saturday evening a couple of years ago and not a word had been spoken for an hour at least. It was that engrossing a drama.

Then, at a lull in the action, Mrs Harper leaned over and said: "You know something?"

"What?"

"I never imagined myself marrying a Norman."

Out of nowhere, a knife was plunged to the very depths of my soul.

You'd think that I'd be used to it by now and, in many respects, I am. I accepted a long time ago that I would never be a ladykiller. You were never going to find me in a white tuxedo at Cap d'Agde, nursing a Martini, eyeing the talent and introducing myself to any fetching sex kitten: "The name's Bond. Norman Bond."

I was never going to be a dictator or despot leading a minor Latin American state to ruin and poverty, but having my devoted people shouting at me as I surveyed my empire from the balcony of the Casa Rosada: "Nor-man! Nor-man! Nor-man!"

I was never going to fall in love with a minor member of the Royal Family and be given a title. No Prince Norman of Donside in the next edition of Burke's.

Mrs Harper is a little more sympathetic now. She has asked (in jest) what I would have liked to have been named instead. And I don't know. I wouldn't want one of those hip modern names, first because they'll be out of fashion in 18 months and, second, because few modern names can stand a mangling by North-east vowels. "Jared! Come doon aff that wa!"

I recall meeting an Aberdeen family abroad one year and the daughter, who was five or six, bore the beautiful French name, Giselle. Unfortunately, the melodic pronunciation of Giselle was beyond North-east Grandma, who was in tow, for she referred constantly to her grand-daughter as Jizzle.

Peer quinie.

Nor would I want that dreadful affectation of having three names at once. You know the sort of thing: Angus John Mackenzie.

It's fine in Gaeldom, where there are half a million Angus Mackenzies and you have to sort them out somehow. That's practical.

But when the candidate lives in a row of semis in Moray, say, and imagines that three names make him sound more Scottish, you have to laugh.

So Mrs Harper wondered if it might be an option for me to do as many others: drop the first name and use the middle.

Hmm.

N. Garibaldi Harper.

It has a certain ring, don't you think?

━━ ━━ ━━ ━━

I've worked with a Gary Cooper and a Carrie Grant. I know a Marlon, a Dymphna and, honestly, a motoring writer called Zog whose dad was an admirer of the one-time king of Albania.

32. NEEDLED ABOUT PAIN

Or why males might not be the braver sex

■■ ■■ ■■ ■■

"It's just that the dog is male and, consequently, affa feart
for himsel. As the vet turned round with the blunt-nosed
syringe, all pretence of canine discipline vanished."

IT HAS been an anfractuous week in the howe. To set the
scene for today's episode, I should explain that Mrs Harper
has a theory than men are big bairns when it comes to pain,
even the big bruisers among us.

I think this is a foul slur on the finest of Scottish manhood. I
believe that wives throughout the northern half of Scotland are
well aware of how stoically we men bear pain or discomfort; how
unfazed we are by the prospect of a visit to the doctor's surgery or
the hospital, and how reluctant we are to take to our beds, even
when suffering horrendous illness.

It's fairly clear, ladies, that if the men had the babies there
wouldn't be any of that bawling and shouting now, would there?
What do you mean, who am I kidding?

Mrs Harper's theory is not limited to human males. She says she
has amassed plenty of evidence that the males of any species are
gey peer craiteries when it comes to needles, knives or rubber
gloves. What happened last Saturday afternoon, I have to
concede, lent weight to her theory.

The two of us and the dog (male) had gone out for our usual
weekend constitutional, timing it between bursts of howe rain. As
we passed the vet's surgery on the way to the riverside park, Mrs

Harper noticed that the surgery door was open and remembered suddenly that the big red beast was due his regular dose of kennel-cough medicine.

Seeing her chance, she bustled across the road, hoping that the vet didn't have his hand up something unseemly or that a beast of some sort stood pop-eyed on the examination table.

All seemed reasonably clear, so she asked if she might make an appointment. The vet proposed getting it over and done with at that moment, as he appeared to have a minor lull between one four-legged cataclysm and another four-legged emergency, so she appeared back outside the surgery door and beckoned me from across the road.

The dog, who had spent the short time we had waited by sizing up the surgery and slowly recalling an assortment of needles, thermometers and rubber-glove smells, showed an unusual reluctance to rise from his sitting position.

Persuaded across the road, he arrived in the surgery and went daft. The vet must have thought he was thoroughly undisciplined, which is untrue. It's just that the assortment of smells in a vet's surgery must be the equivalent of a small boy in a soap shop.

He did as he was told and sat, but his behind and paws were hottering on the lino as if at a gentle simmer, and his head was craning through 290 degrees.

The vet went off to charge the syringe with the medicine, turning his back to the dog while he did so. Those of you who are familiar with dogs will know that a kennel-cough dose is administered not through a needle, but through a blunt squirter up the animal's nostrils.

Our normally placid beast has an abiding horror of this. Mrs Harper says this is not because it's a particularly traumatic procedure or that any vet has been rough with him in the past. It's just that he's male and, consequently, affa feart for himsel.

As the vet turned round, brandishing the blunt-nosed syringe, all pretence of canine discipline vanished.

In the middle of this melee, with the dog's lead twining round my legs and the lino being gouged to destruction as he tried to head for the door, the vet looked at me.

"Could you sit down and hold him between your knees to try to steady him?" he said. "Then put your arms round him to lock him down while I try to get close."

Not sure that my joints were up to such contortions and exertions, I made to sit down on the nearest seat, as I had been told. Just in time, Mrs Harper pointed out that the seat in question was on castors and that, had I completed the manoeuvre and had the dog broken free, I would very likely have been the first recorded instance of North-east man rocketing across parks towards Bennachie at 70mph in a seated position.

While that might not have been very dignified, look on the bright side: I could have broken the office-chair land-speed record and earned my place in history.

Instead, I opted for another seat — a sturdy pre-war mahogany model — sitting against another wall, and I shochled across, rebelling dog in tow, plonked myself down, hauled him to sit between my knees and locked my arm under his chin.

He calmed momentarily while the vet slipped a nylon muzzle on him. Our dog hasn't so much as nipped anyone in his four years, but it's always best to be cautious in trauma.

The vet tilted the dog's head back and bore down with the syringe. To say that what followed was akin to a whirlwind of dervishes and banshees breaking loose would be gross understatement. I've seen spin-driers and pneumatic drills with less vigour.

Had I not been involved myself, I would not have believed that so much struggling could come from a normally placid and passive beast.

As for the vet, it is difficult to aim for two nostrils when they are thrashing from left to right, despite the animal's owners' best efforts to steady them.

However, the vet managed a quick squirt up one tunnel and half a squirt up the other, which he declared sufficient.

Now, here's the rub.

Just as the vet leaned back and slipped the muzzle off the dog, the dog tilted his head back, glowered up into my face and let rip the most enormous sneeze, blowing half his kennel-cough medicine back over me. Having exacted his revenge, he stepped from the surgery as bright and lively as ever. I, meanwhile, had a thumping headache within 15 minutes.

While the dog leaped and bounded and gambolled happily about the riverside park, having forgotten all about his medical encounter just minutes before, my mouth had gone dry, the sky had gone dark and my throat had begun to burn.

Heaven knows what is the active ingredient in kennel-cough serum but, trust me, you don't want to tangle with it.

The headache, dryness and hazy vision persisted for the rest of that evening, despite Mrs Harper's conviction that I was malingering.

Happily, I felt fine after a night's sleep, and the symptoms were but a faint memory by the time I took my place at the kitchen table with my bran flakes the following morning.

Indeed, I'm almost back to normal. The appetite has returned. I'm sleeping well. Best of all, I can now go to kennels nationwide without fear of catching so much as a tickly throat.

Mrs Harper says that she has never seen me looking so healthy in all the time we have been married.

If only I could stop chasing rabbits.

The vet's surgery moved a mile farther away a few months later, but the dog is just as wary of the new place as he was of the old one.

Subsequent attempts to puff medicine up his nose have been marginally calmer but, as a neighbour said, would any of us humans like someone's arm locked under our chin and something cold and wet blown up our beaks?

33. DON'T FORGET THE TIPS

Or why an outstretched palm will become more common

■■ ■■ ■■ ■■

"The best tippers, contrary to national stereotype, were the
Scots. They were just astonishingly generous, particularly
working-class people from the Central Belt."

IT HAS been an oblatory week in the howe. You find me
sitting in the afterglow of a holiday in New England in the
Fall. Since our return at the weekend, I have been marvelling
yet again at the Can Do nature of most of American society. Over
there, they have a lack of the snideness and cynicism which too
many people over here think is smart. You get to admire the
cheerfulness of the customer care in shops, restaurants, banks and
just about everywhere service is required.

Britons who mock the Have A Nice Day culture have failed to
grasp the sincerity behind it, or how quickly it becomes
exceedingly pleasant when you're on the receiving end of all that
courtesy.

There is but one flaw. Many are the US public civilities and
courtesies which I wish would infect us here, but one American
custom is becoming increasingly irritating with each visit.

Tipping.

At a rough estimate, our two weeks in New York and New
England left us £100 lighter for no tangible return. All of that went
in tips.

I'm not so green that I hadn't experienced it already and known
to expect it this time, too. I've been travelling to the US for 20

years, but this was the first time I had noticed that the tipping principle had pervaded life to a degree that had become, frankly, ridiculous.

What possibly can be the reason for a tips jar in a bank? Or in a Starbucks coffee shop? Or a post office?

How does a bank teller change money especially efficiently to merit 10% of the cash back in her polystyrene cup? How does pouring coffee from a glass hotjug into a polystyrene cup and sliding it across the counter at you justify a 50-cent thank-you? If you don't tip the post-office clerk, does she sell you the stamps with particularly nasty gum?

Frankly, my dear, it's a racket. Its a device used by employers who pay pittance wages to gull the public into subsidising their profits — and I speak as someone who has lived on both sides of the tipping fence.

In my school-holiday jobs as a hotel porter in the mid-1970s, I trebled my wages in tips, and very welcome it was, too, for otherwise I would have been earning £9 for a 54-hour week.

But those were tips which were offered (I hope) as a reward for genuine service, and certainly were not expected as a right. The vague prospect of a 10p tip was an encouragement to anticipate the customer's wishes and fulfil them quickly, crisply and efficiently. Sometimes it bore fruit and sometimes it didn't, but we cried no tears and cursed no curses when we drew blanks.

By the way, the best tippers, contrary to national stereotype, were Scots. They were just astonishingly generous, particularly working-class people from the Central Belt.

Next were Scandinavians and Germans, followed by a sequence covering nearly every nation in Europe and most of the Commonwealth. Second from bottom of the tipping league were Americans, believe it or not, presumably overcompensating for being fleeced so shamelessly by their countrymen at home.

Propping up everyone else and earning the 1975 award as the grippiest blighters on the face of the earth were . . . well, I don't like to say, really, but their capital city is London.

No hotel porter I knew minded not getting a tip, but we were amused constantly by the devices which many tourists from south of the border would dream up to avoid parting with a bob when we delivered their cases to their rooms. These included hiding in the en-suite bathrooms, pretending they weren't in the room at all, or rushing away down the lobby as if in a hurry to go for an emergency walk.

One man tried pretending he was Dutch and, consequently, not familiar with British money. Don't ask me why. The only flaw in Jan van Klump's strategy was the label on his case showing he was a Mr Outhwaite or some such from Barnsley.

Had these people known how unnecessary (but entertaining) their wee pantomimes were, I hope they'd have had the sense not to bother. A simple thank-you always sufficed.

How these tip-evaders would have coped in the US has puzzled me often. The answer is that they wouldn't. They would have had to suffer, grimace and squeal as their small change was surgically removed by assorted doormen, hairdressers, taxi-drivers and maitre Ds.

For there is no embarrassment among American hotel porters, doormen or restaurant staff about holding our the flat of the hand. Those hands stay out until paper crosses them. Don't even think that you'll get off with mere coin.

Sign a credit-card chit in a US restaurant and the word TIP with a big blank space beside it is bigger than the type showing the actual cost of the service.

Any Briton who imagines that a tip is discretionary in the States is soon disabused of the notion. Indeed, the latest travel guides and Internet websites all warn America-bound Europeans that tips are more or less compulsory.

I have in front of me a page from an Internet website guide to New York which reads:

". . . and never EVER with-hold a tip, no matter how poor the service has been. You can increase from the basic 15% for good service, but on no account go below."

My brother knows why. When his two boys were smaller, he, my sister-in-law and the two young ones went to a fast-food joint in Florida. The service, apparently, was diabolical; not just slow, but cobweb-inducing. The waitress was not just sullen; a cloud of anger and boorishness hung about her. The food was not just poor, it was concrete.

So they left. And they left without leaving a tip because, being British, my brother made the mistake of assuming that a tip rewarded good service, when it doesn't. It acknowledges the fact that you have been served.

As they strode across the car park to their rental car, they heard the door of the restaurant open. Seconds later, a spew of electric-blue invective blared across the car park at them. He doesn't remember the detail of the waitress's parthian shot, but it involved orifices, other items best left hidden and private activities.

He has since learned his lesson. Just as I fear, given the fact that Britain tends to follow American trends, we will all be learning the ropes of institutionalised tipping here sooner or later.

In which case, we had better be prepared to pay for it.

I will do my bit by getting my polystyrene cup ready for visitors to the front reception at the Lang Stracht.

May I respectfully suggest a going rate of 2p a sentence?

— — — —

> *The sharpest man for wringing tips out of people was Jimmy Hudson, a Glaswegian who knew more about human psychology than any shrink. I used to marvel as Jimmy worked hotel visitors so that they would be positively bursting to hand over fistfuls of small change. He said the key was to make any trivial task seem like it had been an immense burden. The customer was then impressed and grateful, and gratitude and reward would always run in direct proportion.*

34. BACKWARD IN COMING FORWARD

Or why some Scots won't give you more than a couple of words

▬ ▬ ▬ ▬

"Too outgoing and you're an attention-seeker. Too reserved and you're a snob. The middle ground is so narrow that I wouldn't like to try hitting it myself."

I T HAS been an obmutescent week in the howe. One of my newer colleagues, who has just arrived from his native Englandshire, confessed to me the other day that it was a bit of a struggle to get to know the people of northern Scotland.

"It's not that you're cold or anything," he said, "but it's very difficult to keep up a decent conversation when the other end is all one-word answers."

I made light of it, of course, and assured him, as his neighbours studied us from behind twitching net curtains, that this part of Scotland was a very welcoming place.

A woman walking her dog approached and both animal and mistress seemed suddenly to find something supremely fascinating about their feet as they passed. I had the feeling that they would have preferred to have crossed the road, but that only the traffic was preventing them.

"You see what I mean?" said my colleague. "Or am I imagining it?"

At the time, I assured him that he certainly was imagining it and that he should give his new neighbours time to get to know him. He said he had been doing his best to get to know everyone; telling any new neighbour he met in his small village that they were very welcome to drop around at any time, but he had been disappointed to find that in five weeks so far no one had.

I explained that very few older North-east people would trust such an informal arrangement as "pop in any time", and that most would prefer a specific invitation, at least in the early stages.

He didn't seem convinced.

The more I thought about it as I drove home, the more I could see why northern Scotland sometimes might give the wrong impression. It must be exceptionally difficult for an outsider to judge how to hit the right social note.

Too outgoing and you're an attention-seeker. Too reserved and you're a snob. The middle ground is so narrow that I wouldn't like to try to hit it myself. Unless you know how to handle us, the innate reserve could come across as ambivalence, maybe even antipathy.

Of course, sometimes you just have to accept that there are North-east people who will girn and bitch about you whatever you do, so it's best just to laugh quietly at them and carry on regardless.

If it's any consolation to those of you struggling to fit into a new community, the reserve and reluctance sometimes fox us natives, too. A couple of decades ago, I was assigned to head for a cottage in the middle of a small Aberdeenshire hamlet 40 miles or so from Aberdeen.

I'm not going to name it, to spare the embarrassment of anyone who might be extant, but the story involved a retired farm servant who had fallen heir to an old but and ben up in the Banffshire hills. It was a pretty ramshackle agglomeration of stones by all accounts, barely one step up from a cattle shelter, but in a press at the back there had been a grubby painting of a rural scene which he had put to an antiques shop for advice.

The antiques man had been sufficiently honest to spot it as a rare work by an Edwardian artist and had sent it to auction. It had made £18,000, which was a lot of cash in the late 1970s, and it assured the old chap a more comfortable retirement than he might otherwise have had.

What interested our news editor was the paradox of a man who had toiled all his days, and who lived alone in a cottage without indoor plumbing, and with electricity supplied only by an old diesel engine in a shed out at the back, finding suddenly that he was five figures richer with his inheritance of a dilapidated hoosie and a prized painting. Would it change his way of life?

I was dispatched as a young reporter to come back with a good, newsy, colour piece; a feature which conveyed the essence of the man and his sudden good fortune.

I arrived at a home (not the Banffshire inheritance), which had not known a sniff of paint or Windolene for at least 20 years. The window frames were peeling and dingy net curtains hung listless in the lower halves of very small windows.

Inside, flagstones served as the kitchen floor and, if my memory serves, there was still an old black-lead range in which a few embers glowed in the ashes.

The only furniture was a couple of horse-hair, brown-leather chairs on either side of the fire, a zinc bucket filled with kindling and coal, and a wooden square table behind the door, laid with a plasticised flowery tablecloth.

He sat in one of the armchairs, his clae-davie breeks worn shiny and his jacket patched at the elbows. He had a shock of black hair, far more luxuriant and dark than his years would have suggested. His face had that pallor of someone who hadn't ventured outside in a long time, although his eyes were dark and lively. I'd have put him in his late 70s, although I learned in the following few minutes that he was 92.

When I arrived in the room, I was surprised and almost disappointed to find a middle-aged woman wearing a peeny apron in attendance. The whole point of the tale was that this old chap had landed a windfall and lived alone in fairly spartan circumstances.

In the course of the next few minutes, it transpired that the woman was only his neighbour who popped in on him from time to time. Judging by the way she eyed me warily, she was popping in at that particular moment to be sure that the journalist from Aberdeen didn't cosh the old chap over the head and make off with his riches. You know what journalists are like.

And it was all downhill from there. I've met some reserved and clipped people in my time, but nothing to match this chap.

"How much of a surprise did you get when you were told how much the painting was worth?"

"Big."

"What did you think when you were told?"

"Canna mind."

"How long have you lived here?"

"Lang time."

"Do you know what you'll do with all the money?"

"Lord knows."

"You're in for a comfortable retirement, though."

"Maybe."

And so the dry answers continued. For question after question, it was: "Aye", "Couldna say", "Canna mind", or "Lord knows."

Thoughts of a lively colour piece for the paper were dissolving before my eyes. Whenever I tried to corner him into a longer answer, he would just shrug his shoulders and stare at the fire. Not even a "couldna say".

With all my questions exhausted and barely half a page of notebook filled, I must have looked defeated. He glanced at the neighbour and said: "Tea?" And off she trotted to make a pot of tea, leaving us to our awkward silence. We sat there for a moment or two.

"Well," I said, "closing my notebook and sighing, "you could always invest it carefully and you'll make your pile."

He shifted uneasily in his seat and said: "I've got piles."

▬ ▬ ▬ ▬

The old chap died three years later, in 1982 or 1983, and the will logged in court showed that he hadn't been nearly as poor as anyone had imagined. I think his estate ran to £46,000.

35. ROAD RAGE IN ACTION

Or why some people just look funny when they're having a tantrum

■■ ■■ ■■ ■■

"He stamped with that comic walk of a frustrated Warner
Brothers cartoon character, as if unsure what to do next
to demonstrate what an angry fellow he really was."

IT HAS been an irascible week in the howe After more than 20 years of driving, I think I have witnessed my first real example of road rage. I don't mean the usual tooting, flashing lights and aggressive gestures with fingers, because we see that daily day, especially if you live in Aberdeen, where the standard of driving is positively the worst in the country.

I don't mean even the intimidating swerving and cutting in of the "that'll teach you a lesson, mate" variety, whose victims are usually less confident drivers doing the best they can, or just the honest-to-goodness blissfully ignorant.

If you've suffered that and you think that makes you a victim of road rage, you've led a very sheltered life. That's not really road rage. That's more road pique. I mean honest-to-goodness, blow-your-top, turn-purple, get-out-of-your-car-and-boil-with-fury road rage.

Come with me now to one of Aberdeen's arterial routes, where Mrs Harper and I were travelling four days ago. It was reasonably hot and the traffic was not moving especially quickly, so there were many cheesed-off faces in the cars round about us.

It was a weekend and wasn't even a rush hour, so we assumed that the slowness meant that there were roadworks ahead, or maybe that someone had had a minor bump and that a tailback was developing.

We were still musing on the range of possibilities when there was a loud roar from behind us and the white van (cliché, but true) from three places behind jinked to the left, put two wheels on the pavement and stormed past us on the inside.

The brakes squealed and the brake lights flashed as he reached two places in front of us and bored his way back into the queue. In my rear-view mirror, I could see animated conversations in the other cars that the van had just passed. The driver of the car in front, we could see, was a head-shaker; a practitioner of that slow-motion head-shaking to stress his disdain to anyone he hoped was watching.

For the next half-minute or so, we edged forward with the rest of this embattled trickle of traffic until — roar — white-van man was off again.

This time, he managed to steal only a couple of places more, but he didn't jink back into the queue. Instead, he stopped, half on the pavement and half off, jumped out of his cab and, door still flapping, ran round the back of what looked like a small blue Peugeot sitting in the queue ahead of us.

White-van man was podgy chap in his 30s, balding on top but with long, straggly hair which once had been blond but was now salt and pepper. It sprouted in a ring round the base of his napper, which made him look like a boiled egg sitting on a badly made raffia coaster.

A very angry boiled egg, I should add.

He hauled open the Peugeot driver's door and began shouting inside. I can't lip-read and I couldn't make out the detail, but the occasional anglo-saxonism drifted back on the January breeze; several dozen anglo-saxonisms if we are to be strictly accurate, conjugated in almost every form.

Then began the door-slamming. After the seventh or eighth oath (I think it was the present participle, but it might have been the concrete noun), he slammed the Peugeot door shut, then stamped to left and right, still glaring hotly inside the Peugeot.

He stamped with that curiously comic walk of a frustrated

Warner Brothers cartoon character, as if unsure what to do next to demonstrate what an angry, angry fellow he really was.

Devoid of inspiration, he hauled open the Peugeot door once more and started shouting and swearing all over again. It must have been very intimidating for the poor Peugeot driver, who looked to be a young lad in his teens or early 20s. He was cowering back, jaw dropped, to such a degree that he must have been sitting on the handbrake most of the time, desperate to keep as much distance as possible between himself and his assailant.

I guarantee that all the men in the cars behind this little exchange were wondering at that point what they should do if the victim was hauled from the car and the two began a wee tussle on the tarmac.

Then, Chapter Two of van man's verbal abuse at an end, came the second door slam; so fierce that we felt it in our car five places back. More stamping. More glaring.

Blow me, he hauled open the door again and the sequence began from the top once more. This round of slamming the door shut, pacing and glaring, hauling it open again, effing and blinding, then slamming the door happened four times in all.

I can remember thinking that my colleague, the Press and Journal's motoring writer Ken Tarrant, had always told me that Peugeots weren't terribly solid. Well, that one certainly was. A lesser car would have been carted off to the scrappie, ready dissembled, in a couple of dozen buckets.

Steam spent, and with the eyes of several dozen carbound observers on him, white-van man stamped as furiously as he could back to his van, although now he just looked faintly pathetic. He climbed in and roared off down the pavement, blaring his horn all the way, before he turned at the next junction, bounced off the pavement and was gone.

I've been pondering several questions since Saturday afternoon. Why did nobody, myself included, get out to suggest to van man that he calm down? I think you know the answer.

Did van man realise what a public ass he was making of himself? Probably not, or he wouldn't have gone on for as long as he did. He might have intimidated and frightened the Peugeot driver, but everyone else was thinking: "What a strange little performer." What had Peugeot Boy done to cause such upset? We'll never know. He seemed to me to have been behaving perfectly well. Nothing untoward in his driving drew my attention. Whatever his crime was, it couldn't have been major.

Perhaps he had edged forward and closed the bolthole that van man had marked for himself, or something equally worth a hearing at The Hague.

Perhaps, like many other solo travellers, he had been excavating his nostrils in quiet contemplation, and van man, a stickler for hygiene and etiquette, had been deeply upset.

The whole episode might have had nothing to do with motoring at all, of course. Peugeot man might have been a love rival, or have made van man's daughter with child, or have stolen his last Rolo, or have been responsible for any one of a hundred non-motoring traumas that demanded swift and vocal retribution.

It will remain a mystery to all but the two leads; just one of those little frissons on the vast stage of urban Aberdeen life.

Since this column appeared in 1996, I've witnessed many more road-rage incidents. They seem to be growing more common as our inhibitions about making a public display of ourselves break down.

Still, none was quite as spectacular as this one in North Anderson Drive. I like to hope that after the irate van driver roared off, he turned off in the wrong direction and became even more furious with himself.

Neep.

36. QUESTIONS AND ANSWERS

Or why you'll get any reply except the one you really want

▬▬ ▬▬ ▬▬ ▬▬

" A woman hears a question, assesses it for hidden
meaning, then answers the question she thinks will be
asked two questions down the line."

I T HAS been an anacoluthic week in the howe. I want the
husbands and boyfriends among you to try a small
experiment for me. You can try it for a day or for a week, the
period's up to you, but I'm anxious to see if anyone else has
noticed a phenomenon that seems to be afflicting the female of
the species to an increasing degree.

To set the whole thing in context, I had better explain that it all
starts in politics. If you have a good memory, you'll recall the
interview which the BBC's Jeremy Paxman did in late 1995 with
Michael Howard, who was Home Secretary at the time. The
subject was the sacking of the Parkhurst Prison governor, and
trying to identify which treacherous cove had stuck the
metaphorical knife in the man's back.

Mr Howard fancied he would try the standard ploy of all
politicians in a tight corner: bluster, duck, dive, evade and flannel,
but on no account offer a straight answer to a straight question.

Lesser interviewers would have crumpled or would have been
urged by their producers through their earpieces to stop rattling a
locked door and get on to another topic.

Happily, Paxman inhabits another plane. Each time Mr Howard
gave a deliberately obtuse answer, Paxman would ask the same

question, word for word. After the eighth or ninth repetition, you could see a flash of panic across the Home Secretary's face. At one cut, you could catch him looking off to the side, as if hoping that a merciful floor manager might come and rap Paxman's knuckles.

Fourteen times Paxman asked the same question. Fourteen times Howard circled the truth, trying desperately to dress it up in waffle without actually uttering what was becoming increasingly obvious: that the chief knife-wielder had been Howard himself, grossly abusing a politician's remit.

Michael Howard never did answer the question, but it mattered little, for the damage had been done. He left the studio, image tattery beyond repair. Paxman won an award for conducting the political interview of the year. Political observers came to regard the exchange as the interview which declared open season on all politicians, waffling or not.

The nation learned three years afterwards that a technical hitch in the Newsnight control room had delayed the next item in the programme running order, forcing Paxman to fill for six minutes unexpectedly. He said later that all he could think to do was to ask the same question repeatedly and hope, for once, that he didn't get a straight answer.

I think he's being modest about his terrier instincts but, even if he isn't, it's still only a minor blemish on the most savoury political interview broadcast in the last 20 years.

All of which is a long way round to exploring one of the basics of human communication.

Question . . .

. . . followed by answer.

Q. What colour is the sky?

A. The sky is blue.

Easy.

As we've seen already, however, it's not always that simple, especially when you're interviewing a politician or someone shady with something to hide (frequently the same thing). It can be equally challenging (sorry, ladies) when dealing with the distaff side.

So here's the experiment, chaps: without explaining that you're conducting a test, ask a few straight questions of the love of your life and see how often you get an appropriate answer.

I stress "appropriate answer". I don't mean a correct answer, a truthful answer or a prompt answer. I mean just one that fits the question. Just approximately would do. A rough stab.

How many of you recognise exchanges similar to these?

Q. Should I make the tea tonight or will you?
A. Well, the dog needs a walk.

Q. Do you have any first-class stamps on you?
A. They went up to 27p last week.

Q. Did you say Doris went to Stockholm on holiday?
A. We haven't had a postcard from her.

Before I get more letters from readers telling me that I'm always far too hard on Mrs Harper (most of them in handwriting eerily similar to Mrs Harper's, I must say), I'll hasten to add that these aren't her words, although we've had many such non-sequitur exchanges over the past 10 years.

Besides, psychologists will tell you that these exchanges show a fundamental difference between the way male and female brains work — and that they actually reflect great credit on the woman answering the question.

It seems that a man asks a question and expects to get an answer to that question and that question alone. A woman hears a question, assesses it for hidden meaning, then answers the question that she thinks will be asked two questions down the line.

That way, she saves the two of you an awful lot of time, effort and breath, because the answers to the original question, and all the unspoken ones in between, are implied in a cleverly constructed answer.

It's all super-efficient. Or that's the theory. Not much wonder there are communication difficulties between the sexes.

Q. Does the car need petrol?
A. They've stopped that free wine glasses offer at Esso.

I have often wondered if I should broach this subject with Mrs

Harper's mother; find a quiet moment one Saturday morning to inquire gently about my spouse's question-answering past. As a woman of exceptional wisdom, she would surely put my mind at rest.

Thus, on a visit a couple of Saturday's ago, with several years of curiosity eating at my intimmers, I chose my moment.

Mrs Harper had gone off through to her mother's kitchen to make the three of us our morning fly-cup, softie and syrup, leaving me and my mother-in-law facing each other across the room.

But how do you ask your mother-in-law a personal question about her daughter without alarming her? How do you ask her if she ever noticed that your wife, her beloved offspring, replied to questions by giving unrelated answers? How do you ask where her daughter might have picked up this habit, without worrying her needlessly?

You start by easing in with the small talk, that's how.

When she let slip that she had taken an awful liking for thick fruit yogurt, I fixed on that as a likely vein to mine.

"And which is your favourite flavour?" I said.

"Well," she said, " I get four for 99p at the Co-op."

Any journalist has a favourite tale of a difficult interview. Mine comes from interviewing the now-deceased American author of many a romantic blockbuster, Virginia Andrews, at a hotel in Edinburgh.

Every single answer to every question was: "That's a difficult one. I couldn't say." Her publisher's tour co-ordinator told me later that there had rarely been a more difficult or obstructive woman on the company books.

37. BLUNDER AT THE SANDWICH BAR

Or why you should try not to fly off the handle

■ ■ ■ ■

"I was tired. I was ravenous. I'd spent almost a whole
day on the road and I wasn't in the mood for
sullen service in a sandwich bar."

IT HAS been a contumelious week in the howe. I wrote
recently about the nonsense of the modern business theory
that The Customer Is King. The customer is frequently a
chancer, I wrote. I knew I would get chiding letters from readers
saying that the traffic was not one way; that they had endured
appalling service at the hands of shop assistants, waiters or public
services.

That's exactly what happened. There are too many to explore
fully here, and many of the correspondents wouldn't want their
trauma to go into public forum. Suffice to say there's a fast-food
outlet in Aberdeen whose teenage staff need a courtesy course.

There is a shop at Elgin with at least one ex-customer who was
virtually accused of being a fraudster when her credit card was
refused. It turned out later to have been a technical hitch, but that
wasn't discovered until long after the woman was on the verge of
tears about a needlessly public humiliation.

And there are at least two garages which tried to charge £2.50
for windscreen fluid as part of a service, even although the car-
owners had made sure before their cars were delivered for
servicing that the washer bottles were brimming with the correct
dose of water and fluid.

All these tales, and a dozen more, ranged from irritating to traumatic for the people involved and it would be foolish of me to pretend otherwise. The point of last week's column was that the business-customer relationship is rarely black and white. There are rogue elements on both sides of the counter. Since we hear more about the rogues in business, we were trying last week to introduce a wee bit of balance by exploring the phenomenon of customer rogues who fancy they will exploit the better natures of companies and public services.

For the record, I also had half a dozen letters from front-line people in service industries; people who have borne the brunt of customer tantrums and who find their jobs exhausting. The tone of this part of the correspondence was that "dealing with the public would be fine if we didn't have to deal with the public".

I can recall one person in customer service who must be thinking the same. She had to deal with an incredibly irritated customer after she had made a simple mistake.

If it is any consolation to her, the customer has spent the last eight months stricken with remorse. A heat rushes to his face every time he thinks about the incident and he wishes profoundly that it had never happened. The unfortunate assistant was working in the deli-sandwich part of a food court in New England.

The nasty customer? Me.

Even if I try to set this in context, I don't come out of it particularly well. Mrs Harper and I had spent a long day driving across Vermont and New Hampshire. We were tired and ravenous when, lo, there appeared in the East a shopping mall; one of those big jobs with a 20-screen cinema, six filling stations and enough car-park tarmac to cover the whole of Inverness.

These things invariably have huge food courts where the cuisine is not half bad, so we headed for the off-ramp.

Other patrons perhaps thought it odd to see two tourists bounding up the escalators two steps at a time, loud grumbles echoing from their insides, but when ravenous you're not too concerned about public dignity. Mrs Harper headed for the sushi bar and I, more traditional, headed for the deli-sandwich counter.

I studied the various options on the illuminated board above the counter. I was the only customer at that time of night. A blonde of about 17, quite plump, waited for me to step forward and speak. Her intense stare made me feel a little like an exhibit, but eventually I asked for a tuna sandwich, a fruit salad and some water.

She carried on staring as if I were off my head, but she said not a word. Instead, she spun round and began assembling the order. Two minutes later, she dumped it in front of me. I watched as she rang up her till, then handed her a $20 bill. She gave change. The whole exchange had been wordless, almost to the point of being rude.

I was tired. I was ravenous. I'd spent almost a whole day on the road and I wasn't in any mood for sullen service. I said: "Thank you *very* much" and joined Mrs Harper at her table, where she was tucking into some raw-fish meneer that didn't bear close examination.

I always look at the filling in a sandwich before I bite, and it was a good thing I did. The tuna was turkey. Not only had I been treated sullenly, I hadn't even got what I wanted.

"Just eat it," said Mrs Harper. "They're closing up."

But, no. Instead, I strode back to the counter and waited until the girl showed herself again. "I wanted tuna," I said. "This is turkey." She was staring again, then she stared down at the sandwich. She swept it away.

Presently, a man in shirt and tie appeared, apologised and asked me to go back to my seat. The correct order would be delivered without delay.

I went back and was waiting with increasing impatience when Mrs Harper said: "Look at what's happening behind the scenes."

The manager was giving the girl a telling off. There was no finger wagging, but the body language was clear. I can't say I was disappointed.

Thirty seconds later, the girl appeared at my table with my sandwich and began to apologise. As soon as she began speaking, I wished a hole could have opened and swallowed me.

The lassie was deaf.

She apologised that she had been staring, but that was because she had been lipreading. She apologised that I had been given the wrong sandwich, but she had thought genuinely that I had said turkey, not tuna. She apologised that she had not spoken at the counter, but she didn't like to speak if she could help it, because people thought her laboured speech curious.

Then, in a coup de grace which I knew she didn't intend, she said quietly: "Enjoy your meal," and walked slowly back to her job.

If I say I felt two inches tall for the rest of the holiday, that would be overestimating it by an inch and a half. Even now, I feel a heat rising in my face.

Mrs Harper says I make too much of it; that I hadn't been rude in the least; that I was merely correcting a mistake in an order; that I had no way of knowing that the person was deaf, and that a deaf person would be grossly insulted to think they were being pitied.

But I wasn't pitying her. I was embarrassed for myself and the Size15 feet I had stuck in my mouth of my own volition. The lassie got a dressing-down when she had only been doing her best.

And I have even more reason to believe that the clarion "The Customer Is King" is nonsense. The customer is frequently Mr Clod.

Several readers, many of them deaf or hearing-impaired, wrote to say that I shouldn't have felt bad about this and that someone serving the public should expect to be disciplined for not doing a job properly, irrespective of disability.

I'm still not so sure. She seemed to take it in her stride, but I still kick myself for having been so quick to fly off the handle.

38. STUFF YOU'LL NEVER NEED

Or how to identify the rubbish masquerading as gadgetry

■■■ ■■■ ■■■ ■■■

"A CD player in the shower. Is there not enough noise
in the world without your morning ablute being
adulterated, too?"

I T HAS been a detrital week in the howe. I'm obliged to the
oil-industry executive who was inspired by last week's
column on useless gadgets. He sent me a sales catalogue
which he had lifted from the seatback on a flight he took in the
Deep South of the US last week. I'm obliged to him because
leafing through the 172-page Skymall clubbie book makes all the
junk in my garage look worthwhile.

"Even allowing for the fact that a captive audience on a flight is
prone to the madness inspired by unnatural surroundings and will
happily pay good money for trash," he wrote, "it seems a little
ambitious of the publishers to try to persuade otherwise sane
passengers to part with cash for some of this nonsense."

Having perused the catalogue at some length, I find it hard not
to agree.

What could possibly be the point of a radio-controlled meat
thermometer? This is an $89 device by which you stick an eight-
inch heat-resistant transmitter probe into your Sunday joint and
can then walk away up to 75ft, confident that the minute your
roast is threatened, a bleeper in your pocket will go off.

If your Sundays are so hectic that you can't look in on a roast
every 10 minutes without the order of your household collapsing

about your lugs, you need greater help than an $89 transmitting thermometer can offer.

Then there's a 2ft kitchen wastebin in stainless steel. It looks pretty much like any other kitchen pedal bin except that this one costs $259. Yes, £185 for a kitchen bucket. Why does the Vipp Pedal Bin cost £185, when any normal four-gallon bin would cost about £25? The Vipp has a patented whisper gasket and air brake, so the lid closes with a whuff, rather than a clunk.

How about a cruet set for $139? For your money you get not just an ordinary salt mill and pepper mill, you get electrically powered ones so you don't have to bother with all that nasty twisting. That's so much more stylish than what everyone else seems to do; pinching a set of plastic shakers every time you visit a Little Chef.

Can I interest you in a CD player for $190? The unique selling proposition of the CD Companion (registered trade mark) is that it has been designed specifically for use in the shower. No more boring soaping up and rinsing off in silence. Now you can lather to Schubert, foam to Faure and rinse to Rimsky-Korsakov. I suppose you dry off to Dvorak, but a towel isn't included.

A CD player in the shower. Is there not enough noise in the world without your morning ablute being adulterated, too?

Pets aren't forgotten. The Sta-fresh Drinking Fountain is a $60 attachment for the side of your cat's water bowl. This is a battery-powered device which sucks up the undrunk water and spouts it back from a height of six inches. The theory is that it keeps the water tasting fresh, and "the tinkling noise encourages the cat to drink more often, thus preventing dangerous feline dehydration".

This would be the same tinkling noise that will have every human in the household queueing outside the loo.

The Bug-be-Gone is a $50 hand-held vacuum cleaner (14,000rpm) designed specifically to suck wasps, bees, flies, daddy longlegs and other beasties off your window sill and jam them on to an enclosed sticky block of insecticide and kill them. No mess. No waste. No fuss. No compassion.

The Park-o-Stop is a $20 polythene mat with a bump across its middle (two for $30). The theory is that you place them at a strategic point on your garage floor, a few feet from the back wall.

When you drive into the garage, you keep driving until you feel the bump under your front wheels and then you stop. Hey presto, no damage to your front bumper and no damage to your garage wall. Yes, you could just learn to drive properly, but why stamp on the sort of product innovation evident in Park-o-Stop?

If you'll allow me to digress for a moment, I was told lately of an Aberdeen company director who owns one of the latest BMWs with sonar parking. This is a system whereby sensors in the bumper use sonar to measure the distance from car to obstacle.

The closer you get to an obstacle, the faster the beeps in the cabin. When the beeps become continuous, you stop. Simple — and brilliant for those awkward parking challenges.

Our hero decided to demonstrate the new gadget to one of his neighbours. He invited the neighbour to hop into the passenger seat and began reversing towards a low wall, confident that the bleeping would start the minute the wall presented a threat.

Long before the bleeping even started, there was a bang and a crunch. Result? Several hundred pounds of damage to a week-old executive saloon. Lesson? Radar parking is marvellous for warning of low walls and other cars, but it hasn't been trained to look out for iron gate barriers at the height of the boot lid.

Had the BMW-owner in question been a golf enthusiast (aren't they all?), he might have taken his mind off his inflated insurance bill with the Aqua Shot. This is a floating golf hole. Yes, a floating golf hole. It's a piece of heavy-gauge black plastic with a small yellow flag poking out of a cup-sized hole in the centre.

You float it in your swimming pool (what swimming pool?) and pitch from the edge of the pool towards the floating hole in the middle. The advantage here is that you never lose the ball. Sadly, you get extremely wet retrieving it, but why look for the flaws in every theory?

What do you suppose the Alderwood Pen-hold Box could be? It's a box made from alderwood for holding pens. Why anyone would want to spend $69 on a glass-fronted display case for Biros, even a case with a "matte-silver pull handle", escapes me for the moment, but it would be a sad world if we all had the same curious foibles.

But my favourite has to be the Aladdin Power-a-Phone if only because it combines two of the scourges of the modern consumer society. Have you ever been talking on your mobile when the tell-tale beeps have interrupted to warn you that the power was running low, and there you were in the middle of a conversation to secure a multi-million-pound deal for your company?

(What do you mean, you haven't? Enter the spirit of the thing, at least.)

Bring on the Aladdin Power-a-Phone ($75).

This is a fist-sized portable generator. It looks like a giant silver clothes peg with a cord from one end. As the phone power expires, you whip this gadget from the inside of your jacket pocket, plug the wire into your phone, and begin opening and closing the clothes peg to generate enough power to finish your conversation.

According to the bumff, you can operate it one-handed if you need to take notes.

So there you are in the airport, phone jammed on your shoulder, note-taking with your right hand and squeezing like billy-o with your left.

All you need is a pair of cymbals and a drum and you're away.

In subsequent letters from readers came news of a battery-powered pooper-scooper for whipping away dog mess. We're surely not so delicate that we can't use an ordinary plastic bag, are we?

There was also a device for re-texturing toothbrushes. It cost £39.95, according to my correspondent, which would buy an awful lot of toothbrushes.

39. AN EVENING IN CASUALTY

Or how to while away the hours and hours and hours

▬▬ ▬▬ ▬▬ ▬▬

"Imagine the most hectic episode of Casualty you've seen
and then multiply it by four. That's more like an evening
in the genuine article."

IT HAS been a vitiated week in the howe. There has been a
little mischanter since last we spoke, you and I. Mrs Harper
had been poring over colour charts, fabric swatches and paint
cards one Sunday afternoon, trying to work out a new colour
scheme for one of the bedrooms.

She had pondered pinks, considered cobalts, meditated over
magnolia and ruminated over rust.

She had tried so many colour combinations without finding the
right one that her head had begun to swim, so she had decided to
do what she always does when she's feeling the need of a head-
clearing; she went for a stroll with her favourite masculine hunk
(the dog).

She was barely 50yd from the front door when she went over
her ankle. She managed to hirple back to the house, with an
extremely disgruntled dog feeling that he had been short-changed,
and phoned me on my mobile.

By the time I got home that evening, the ankle had swollen to
twice its size and she could put no weight on it.

"What does it feel like?" she said, aiming it at me. As I made to
palpate the offending article, she said: "No, don't touch it," which
left me in something of a quandary. I decided to call the doctor.

The upshot was that we found ourselves in the Accident and Emergency Department of Aberdeen Royal Infirmary at 10pm on a Sunday night.

I had forgotten quite how exotic A&E could be. My last visits there were in the 1970s in a professional capacity when, as occasional late man (the duty reporter who covered 11pm-4am), I would take a traivel round the city in the company of a driver, seeing what was what. A&E was always fertile ground.

I know that A&E staff are somewhat dismissive of the BBC1 drama Casualty, because they feel it doesn't convey an accurate picture.

From what Mrs Harper and I saw on that Sunday evening, I take their point. Imagine the most hectic episode of Casualty you've seen, then multiply it by four. That's more like it.

We introduced ourselves at reception and took a seat. There were a dozen other people sitting glumly when we arrived, all of them scanning us and every one of them, we could tell, worrying that Mrs Harper's injuries might be sufficiently serious to permit her to jump the queue. That's the thing about A&E: they don't call it the waiting area for nothing.

Once we had settled in and had conveyed to our fellow-patients the subliminal message that we were no threat, I felt able to take in our surroundings.

To my left was an elderly woman in a purple anorak and jogging bottoms. She was slumped forward, her head in her hands. Occasionally, she would moan softly.

In front were three large people who were virtually camped at the snacks machine. This was the first family of chain junkfood-eaters I have encountered. No sooner was one bag of salt and vinegar dispatched than another bag was hauled from the depths of the vending machine. If it wasn't crisps, it was nuts. If it wasn't nuts, it was chocolate, or sweeties, or fizzy drinks.

A nurse appeared at one point several hours later and I could hear a hushed discussion. The line that stuck in my memory was the man saying: "She's a bittie breathless." If I had barely stopped all evening between mouthfuls of Golden Wonder, Twix and Tango, I'd have been a bittie breathless myself.

To my right was a very prim woman who was clearly uncomfortable at being there and who looked round disdainfully at what she thought was society's late-night dregs.

Opposite her was a brosey soul, obviously in from the country, with that cheery outlook of a rural wifie who treats everything as just another obstacle to be surmounted.

She was knitting. Periodically, she would catch my eye and smile. It happened so often that I wondered if I knew her. I still don't know if I did or did not.

For half an hour or so, the place was quiet, but then the fun began. A woman who was vomiting into a bucket arrived, accompanied by a man shouting: "She's taen a overdose. She's taen a overdose."

The whole medical and admin staff moved with commendable speed, as if working to a well-rehearsed script. It still wasn't quick enough for the accompanying male, who marched around being not particularly useful and shouting: "This is pathetic. This is pathetic."

If ever there was a candidate for a good clap in the lugs, this fellow was that candidate.

Attention shifted soon to a couple of kilted students, who had clearly been out for a merry evening's entertainment and one of whom had had a contretemps with something sharp.

At least these weren't belligerent in their drink. In fact, they were at that lightly squiffy stage when they were entertaining. "Last time I was in a hospital," the injured party announced to the reception staff, but in a stage whisper, "a doctor smacked my backside."

"And if ye dinna sit doon and behave yersel, son," said the vending-machine man through a mouthful of smokey-bacon flavour, "ye'll get the same again."

So the lads grinned and found two adjacent seats opposite us and sat down.

A few moments later, Mrs Harper nudged me, then nodded across to where the two young kilties were seated, chatting. Let us say only that it was clear, by quite an impressive margin, that they were true Scotsmen.

I tried clearing my throat to draw their attention and warn them, but they were too deep in conversation and too high on youth and the elixir of life to pay any attention to me.

I looked along to my left to see if anyone else had spotted this dramatic turn of events.

The elderly woman in the purple anorak and jogging bottoms certainly had. She had stopped holding her head in her hands and moaning softly. Now she was sitting upright and beaming (although still moaning softly).

In the four hours that we were there, we saw many human stories: the man clad only in his Y-fronts looking for a light for his roll-up; the two bobbies trying to control two fighting women in their 40s; the boy who couldn't get his roller skates off, and the drunk who couldn't get past the first line of: There is a Rose in Spanish Harlem — several dozen tuneless times.

I know the sentiment is done to death, but heaven knows how (or why) people who work in A&E thole the rest of us. I certainly couldn't.

Mrs Harper hadn't broken her ankle, by the way, although the ligaments were torn severely and she'll be on industrial-strength Tubi-grip until Christmas.

But look at the bright side. The bruising is a lovely shade of mustard, lilac and green.

We have our bedroom colour scheme at last.

▬ ▬ ▬ ▬

Every single incident in this column was perfectly true. People who work in Casualty tell me that the evening I described was actually a reasonably quiet and civil night, in which case we're thankful that we weren't there during a rush or a riot.

40. GIVE ME A SIGN

Or why reading between the lines doesn't help

■■ ■■ ■■ ■■

"The waitress said nothing, but took the menu from the customer's grasp, flipped it over and tapped a line of type on the front cover."

IT HAS been a glozed week in the Howe. I had been hoodwinked into accompanying Mrs Harper on our latest trawl for the weekly groceries. On these occasions, I am chief trolley-pusher and deputy comestible-gatherer, which leaves me plenty of time to gaze vacantly into the middle distance before the discreet clearing of a feminine throat hauls me a couple of steps farther down the aisles.

It was on one of these daydreaming pitstops at the weekend that I spotted a sign that shook me from my reverie. It was quite a big cardboard job, suspended from the ceiling, and it read:

For our discerning customers

Underneath was a chill cabinet full of obscure stuff from the four corners of the globe that I would doubt would find room in any self-respecting Scottish larder. The contents of that deli shelf weren't the point, however. It was the sign.

If that chill cabinet contained stuff for the store's discerning customers, what sort of customer was frequenting the rest of the store? Some of them did look a bit haunted and exotic, right enough.

By the time Mrs Harper caught up with me, I was craning round, looking well beyond head height to see what the other signs read. As she tumbled assorted vegetables and fruit into the trolley, she sighed and said: "What's the trouble now?"

"I'm looking for a sign."

"What sign?"

"One that reads:

For our empty-headed clientele

or maybe

For all you tinks and minkers

She just walked off towards the carrots, evidently not wanting to explore the darker recesses of a troubled mind.

The supermarket sign was just the latest evidence of the minefield that exists for the retail trade when it comes to dealing with members of the public.

I had a letter not so long ago from a Ross-shire woman who had ventured to Aberdeen for a weekend break with her sister and brother-in-law. They had repaired to a restaurant that had aspirations to be a cut above everything else in the city and which had been decorated accordingly in the latest mode. I know the establishment in question and, yes, the cutting-edge design makes it a bit severe and unwelcoming.

The management had obviously twigged that the look of the place was perhaps putting off a large sector of the potential custom so, to try to broaden their lunchtime trade, they had put an A-board on the pavement outside to explain that families were welcome. The chalked script read:

Children served

My correspondent told me that a waitress seated them at table and presented their menus. Five minutes later, the waitress returned and took the two women's orders, then turned to the man of the party. He ordered an onion ring starter, then said: "And for my main course, I'd like an eight-year-old, medium-rare, with a side-salad."

The waitress paused, pencil hovering, and looked round at the party, unsure of what was going on. "Oh, all right," said the man, shutting the menu. "If you're out of eight-year-olds, give me a couple of four-year-olds. Just don't cook them for so long."

He made do with vegetarian lasagne.

We've all heard the hoary old joke about the man wandering aimlessly round the bottom of an escalator trying to find a dog because a sign read:

Dogs must be carried

I've also been led to believe — although I can't get tale corroborated — that our lower standards of literacy in Scotland these days led to a hastily scrawled sign outside the restaurant marquee at an agricultural show this summer. The sign read:

No smoking aloud

I hope someone had the wit to ask a steward if it was all right to smoke quietly.

But it's restaurants that appear to have the most problems with signs and warnings. Another correspondent wrote to the Press and Journal several years ago to complain about the way she and her family had been treated in a cafe in Aberdeen.

Passage of time renders the memory more faint than I would like so I hope I recount the tale accurately, but I think our reader had her elderly mother with her. The old lady had not much of and appetite, so her daughter asked if it would be all right if her mother had had a half-portion of whatever dish took her fancy.

The waitress said nothing, but took the menu from the customer's grasp, flipped it over and tapped a line of type on the front cover. The message read:

No half portions

There then followed a long debate about the waste of food and waste of money. Ultimately, the woman said that she was quite prepared to pay the full-meal price, but that putting a full portion of food on her mother's plate would inevitably lead to waste.

The waitress was unmoved, which was the point that I would have been handing the menus to her and reaching for my coat.

But the discussion carried on for a couple minutes more until it reached an impasse. And in that awkward silence, the waitress said. "You can't have a half-portion, but you could have a child's portion if the manager says it's OK."

"What's a child's portion?" asked our reader.

You've guessed it. A child's portion was half an adult's portion.

Who says that the Scottish tourist trade is its own worst enemy?

But my favourite tale of a public sign or inscription is actually a joke. Much as I would like it to be true, I have no evidence it is.

It concerns a Buchan man who had a morbid fascination with death and funerals. His wife had thought it engaging in the early days of her marriage, but then it became slightly creepy.

Still later, it began to annoy her, particularly when they both got to that age when people's thoughts turn to their own funerals.

At every opportunity, he would explain his latest views on how their funeral services might run; whether they would be buried or cremated, and so on and so forth.

Then, one day, he asked her over breakfast what she would like on gravestone. "I haven't a clue," she said, but he urged her to think about it for a moment, so she said drily.

"Just make it say:

Wife of the above

▬ ▬ ▬ ▬

I'm told there's a Glasgow store which has a sign:
Crocodile handbags: for every self-respecting
crocodile about town

174

41. PAIN OF A HEALTHY FUTURE

Or why mystery packages aren't always good things

▬ ▬ ▬ ▬

"After the ease of the first few turns of the pedals, my calves felt as if they had been twisted off and my knees had no power or feeling."

IT HAS been an agonistic week in the howe. A large, brown-cardboard carton appeared in the back sitting-room one day recently. It was unmarked, which meant either that it had fallen off the back of a lorry or that it was none of my business.

You may take it that it was none of my business.

Despite my best efforts to prise a few clues from Mrs Harper, the lady wasn't for spilling. Thus, I assumed that the box contained a Christmas gift. Since it was rather a large box, I hoped that it contained my rather large Christmas gift. As every seven-year-old knows good things don't come in small packages, they come in really huge ones.

I had resigned myself to waiting, unknowing, for a further five weeks, perhaps giving the box a kick, tap or comprehensive shoogle now and again for clues when no one was looking.

But then one evening Mrs Harper appeared at my side with a screwdriver and a set of spanners. I made the mistake of looking up and had them thrust into my lap.

"There you go," she said. "Set to work."

I could spin you a long yarn about how I played it very cool and left the job until the weekend, or that I cut open the carton with my Stanley knife to be confronted by an incomprehensible jumble of parts. Instead, I'll tell you that 27 seconds later it became clear that I was looking at a self-assembly exercise bike.

Mrs Harper has been threatening me with an exercise bike for several months now, mainly because I don't take any exercise. Lifting the Roget's is my stretch these days, which is bad, I know.

I had to admire her confidence, however, because she knows perfectly well that I have ridiculed exercise bikes and their users in the past. If you're going to expend all that energy, you might as well go somewhere, see something and get a few midgies in your teeth. Buying an exercise bike unilaterally was a substantial risk.

It wasn't so much of a risk these days, however. The era when the back roads of the howe saw a tractor once an hour and a passing car was a social event are long gone. Nowadays, with so many commuters at full pelt, you'd need to be off your nut to venture anywhere on two wheels hereabouts. Heaven knows how cyclists cope in big, sophisticated places such as The Toon.

So I set to work assembling the exercise bike to the best of my limited ability to wield a spanner, a screwdriver, a torque wrench, pliers and a flashie all at the same time, while reading a one-page instruction sheet translated from Chinese first into Finnish and only then into English.

Try this, for example:

"Step 7. Repeating Step 1 with only four of part B32 assembling from the backwards, make sure all bolts are alignated truly. Offering up Unit F to hole C3. Push to well. Lock with snap and turn against clockwise. Please not to tighten too much (see Step 9). If too much tight return to Step 4 and release sub-assembly from bracing base, before to begin newly."

The whole leaflet was phrased like that. You won't be surprised to know that after three and a half hours of DIY practised at the limit, I reached the last step in the instructions. Back aching, eyes sore, I stood up to survey my handiwork, and there it was.

A hatstand.

All right, it wasn't a hatstand, but it didn't look very much like an exercise bike, either. Imagine a Frisbee tipped up on its side, with two stirrups at either flank and, protruding from the top, a painfully small-looking sponge-foam seat on the end of a pole.

I have been assured since that this was the latest word in exercise bikes. The Frisbee contained a score of high-powered magnets which simulated the pedalling resistance of going uphill.

While the Frisbee might have enclosed the last word in modern exercise technology, it wasn't the magnets which concerned me; it was the extremely thin-looking seat atop the wobbly and sharp-looking metal spike that made me apprehensive.

One enthusiastic crunk too many, or a single slack bolt in the seat assembly (see Step 9D), and I wouldn't have needed any help whatsoever in getting uphill.

After several further attempts to get various sub-assemblies "alignated" and Bolt F4 threaded through Nut K8, we had what looked like a reasonable approximation of an exercise bicycle. Now all we needed was a test pilot.

Affecting sundry aches and pains after four hours of DIY, I stood back graciously and offered Mrs Harper the debut trip to nowhere. She clambered aboard, grasped the handles and, immediately, the dashboard lit up.

I hadn't come across a bike with a dashboard before, but this one illuminated like a car's instrument panel, with readouts of distance covered, calories used, time spent, pulse rate and other such useful things. And off she went. Pretty soon, according to the instrument panel, she was bowling along her imaginary highways and by-ways at 20mph.

The dog and I stood and watched this pseudo-journey for a few moments; the dog a little less impressed than I. Eventually, once he had jaloused that he wasn't actually being taken anywhere and that he couldn't trot alongside, he gave up and sloped off to his basket. I, meanwhile, stood by ready to cope with imminent cardiac arrest.

When she finished, 10 minutes later, her face was slightly flushed, but her breathing was changed hardly at all. She was evidently much fitter than I thought. I suspect she was much fitter than even she thought, for she looked, puzzled, at the dashboard then beamed and reached for a towel.

"Now you," she said.

I couldn't let down my sex, so I climbed aboard a little more enthusiastically than was warranted. I hammed it up for the first 100 yards or so, offering royal waves and cheery hellos to imaginary passers-by. But you know how marathon runners report that they hit "the wall" somewhere around 15 miles, when all their little accoutrements and extremities feel as if they're going to seize, and the aching becomes so intense that they feel like collapsing?

My "wall" hit at around three minutes. After the ease of the first few turns of the pedals, the fronts of my thighs gradually felt numb. My calves felt as if they had been twisted off and my knees had no power or feeling.

"Still fine?" Mrs Harper said.

"Just going up to the top road," I puffed. "That last corner's a bit of a challenge."

"It's good for you," she said. "We'll soon have you capering about like a spring lamb."

Ladies and gentlemen, only male pride kept me pedalling that contraption. I never made it to the top road. I barely made it out of the howe. My thighs, knees and calves are only just recovering. My behind felt for days as if it had been given a good skelping.

I have not been aboard again. Mrs Harper, however, has travelled half of Scotland, judging by the trip meter.

One evening, I'm going to turn the resistance switch up to maximum when she's not looking.

███ ███ ███ ███

> *The exercise bike had to be returned not long after this column appeared. It transpired that using it was so strenuous because it had only one gear — uphill.*
>
> *Yes, there were nine different settings on the gear lever, but each one was the same as the other, and my little leggies couldn't take it.*

42. IMAGE AND REALITY

Or why some people can't help jumping to conclusions

▄▄▄ ▄▄▄ ▄▄▄ ▄▄▄

"I have consoled myself with the thought that journalists
weren't born to be popular. If we're not rubbing someone
the wrong way, we're not doing the job properly."

IT HAS been an adumbral week in the howe. I'm a little hurt this morning. You'll have seen the results of the survey, conducted in six European countries, Australia and the US, in which more than 22,000 respondents declared which profession they trusted most and which they trusted least.

Up at the top were nurses (but not doctors), the clergy, school-patrol officers (but not teachers) and airline pilots.

Down around the bottom — and this is the hurtful bit — were journalists. Only lawyers and politicians were viewed with more suspicion. Even estate agents, those masters of hyperbole and fulsome promise, scored marginally better than scribes.

I have tried consoling myself with the thought that journalists aren't born to be popular. If we're not rubbing somebody the wrong way, we're not doing the job properly because we're allowing all manner of dark doings to stay secret.

That's why many newspapers count the number of threatening letters and spluttering phone calls they receive as a measure of success.

But that doesn't wash in this case because it wasn't a popularity survey; it was a survey of trustworthiness, a different (and more damning) thing entirely.

I have also tried consoling myself with the thought that surveys are trite in the extreme. They encourage lazy journalism by dressing up cheap nonsense and allowing it to masquerade as information, thus giving sponsoring businesses a chance to have their products and services mentioned free of charge throughout the media.

Cunning, eh?

But no score here, either; the trustworthiness survey wasn't a commercially sponsored project. It was done by an association of universities and colleges as some sort of international psychology exercise. There was no profit motive at all.

So might the flaw be the size of the survey sample? To poll just 22,000 people out of eight entire countries and claim the result as definitive seems like a remarkable leap of logic.

Except that many pre-election surveys in this country, claimed to be equally definitive, run on samples of 1,000 interviews or fewer.

By now, you'll be coming to much the same conclusion as I have done. Despite my best efforts to trawl for excuses, journalists' image is not quite as shiny bright as it might be.

This has led to some awkward moments in the past. I remember, back in my days as a reporter, being sent to a small Deeside village to see what I could find out about a woman who had disappeared.

When I say "a small Deeside village", I mean a village so small that the 30mph signs were almost back to back.

Trying to find guidance and information was clearly going to be a challenge. In the absence of any shops, I did what any sensible newshound would do and headed for the hotel.

It was deserted, too. I dinged the bell at the wee green-baize card table that passed for the Reception. I called: "Hello" several times in case someone mistook me for a miscreant, and poked open a swing door to the area behind the scenes.

I could hear voices in the distance so, still calling: "Hello", I headed towards them.

Eventually, the voices stopped. I pushed open the door to the hotel kitchen and there sat two middle-aged women, newsing at a table and nursing a cup of tea each. I explained my business and the reaction was swift. Both stood up. One reached for a brush to wave at me. The other snorted: "Your sort's nae welcome here. Get oot." Clearly, they were good judges of character.

"You reporters cause enough misery," said one as she rounded the table. I think the word vultures might have featured somewhere.

Had I stayed long enough to be battered about the ears by Betterware's best, I feel sure the two of them would have played the anti-Press lobby's perennial trump card and begun berating me for harassing the Royal Family, but I made my excuses and left a good deal more hastily than I arrived.

Even now, more than 20 years later, I recall the incident vividly, especially when I drive past the hotel, as I do two or three times a year.

I can only conclude that someone in the women's ken had had a court case recounted at length on Page Three of the Press and Journal and that they hadn't much cared for the due process of transparent justice. Their reaction was too extreme and too sudden for anything else.

As the first Pressman to stumble into their coven, I became a prime target for their vengeance, and only some nifty footwork past the aspidistra and the hallstand and out into the street saved me from a matching pair of cauliflower lugs.

You get used to that. People are funny that way.

Once or twice, I have found myself smiling in cafes or restaurants as groups of people at a nearby table have been devouring the latest grubby scandal in one of the less reputable tabloids.

Often, the paper has been disassembled into a multitude of sheets so that various parts of the scandal can be read in concert, then passed on in a sort of titillation round-robin.

When all in the group have absorbed every scrap of filth, and they have sat back, faces flushed, breathing heavily and utterly sated after a full 10 minutes of intensive, pop-eyed reading, you may be sure that someone will say: "It's disgustin printin stuff like that."

I mention that not to defend the printing of salacious tripe in the tabloids, but to point out that there's a market for everything, even when that target market doesn't like to think of itself as the most eager participant in the game.

That's why the tabloids have become obsessed with the Royal Family — to a ridiculous degree, in my view.

My last Royal assignment was going to Upper Deeside one dreich November day several years ago to soak up the atmosphere on the Princess Royal's second wedding.

The memory that will live with me for years is not the convoy of Range Rovers or the light spilling from Crathie Kirk, but the assembly of gawpers and tourists, many with binoculars, stools and flasks of tea, telling any reporter who hauled out a notebook that it was high time the Royal Family was left alone.

Irony wasn't their strong suit, evidently.

Still, however low journalists' standing in the international popularity stakes might be, I can always take comfort from the fact that, even at our lowest, we're not scraping the bottom of the league. That honour goes to lawyers.

Which brings me to the latest joke doing the rounds in Scottish legal circles.

Q. What's black and white and looks good on a solicitor?

A. A pitbull terrier.

One of the strange things about working for a newspaper is that complete strangers meet you at a function and become belligerent to the point of being downright rude.

You never know if it's because they were once up in court and it was reported in the Press and Journal, or if their charity fund-raiser didn't get publicity, or any one of 101 other minor slights. The word "journalist" is a red rag to some people.

43. WHAT WAS THAT AGAIN?

Or why verbal stumbles can be great entertainment

■■ ■■ ■■ ■■

"As she handed the multipack of Bounty bars to me,
she confided: 'I canna thole Bountys. Desecrated coconut
gets aneth my teeth.' "

IT HAS been a neoteristic week in the howe. This week, I
received one of my quarterly letters from someone who was
a neighbour when I used to live in Aberdeen. She was a
smashing lady, of pensioner vintage, and relentlessly helpful to a
young bachelor about town who hardly knew his way round an
iron, let alone an ironing board.

When, after five years, I decided that the call of the howe was
growing too strong and I moved back to my roots (all 25 miles
away), she insisted that we kept in touch.

We all say that, don't we?

No idle promise this, though. She really has kept in touch. Since
1989, she has penned three or four letters a year and has
continued even now that she has moved to live with her son and
daughter-in-law in Warwickshire.

She has two great talents as a letter-writer. First, I know
absolutely no one who appears in her letters, but she is so adept
at painting word pictures of her family, neighbours and friends,
and their little habits and foibles, that she makes them come alive
on the page as individual characters. She's an unwittingly
entertaining writer who would put many professionals to shame.

Second, and I know she won't mind me saying this, she

sometimes stumbles upon the wrong word, with deeply comic effect. It happens in her writing now as it used to happen in her conversation when we lived near each other in the mid-1980s.

For instance, she was the first person I heard talk, in hushed tones, of senile dementia as Aul Timers' Disease.

She mentioned once that she had such profound respect for Sir Winston Churchill that, when he died in early 1965, she insisted that her husband and she would take the train to London to file past the coffin and pay their respects.

"It was awful moving," she told me quietly. "Just a pale light, four soldiers and Mr Churchill's coffin lying on a catapult."

She once presented me with a multipack of Bounty bars because, she said, she knew I liked chocolate. She admitted that she wasn't the one who had bought them: a visitor had given them to her because he had assumed, erroneously in this case, that all old people liked a sweetie.

As she handed them to me, she confided: "I canna thole Bountys. Desecrated coconut gets aneth my teeth."

A former colleague used to receive long, rambling letters from her mother-in-law in New Zealand. Although the letters were warm and entertaining, there was never much structure to them, said my colleague. From the look of it, ideas popped into the woman's mind and were poured immediately on to paper in a newsy and gossipy stream of consciousness.

As a result, the thread of the letters became increasingly difficult to follow as different topics barged in, shot off at tangents, doubled back, disappeared for a paragraph or two and resurfaced in a completely unrelated passage.

Periodically, the author would realise that she had drifted from her theme and, helpfully, would write: "But there I go transgressing again."

The most comic of all malapropisms, of course, are the ones uttered by people who imagine themselves to be just a little finer than the rest of us yet who, in unguarded moments, show that they are just as fallible as everyone else.

Someone who was at school with me in the early 1970s wrote recently to reintroduce herself now that she was back in the

North-east after several years abroad with her husband and his company. She recounted that when her husband was still her husband-to-be and was introduced to her mother, the meeting was not particularly comfortable.

"All mothers want the best for their daughters, but mine wasn't even prepared to see that the best was the best," she wrote. "She was very clipped about the whole thing, and my husband doesn't mind admitting now that he was sweating by the time he left.

"When he had gone, the atmosphere in the house was so thick that you could have cut it. It was one of those heavy silences that meant you just knew something was about to explode. Eventually, I said: 'So, what did you think of him? Isn't he nice?'

"There was a disdainful snort and she brushed past me. 'You maybe think so.'

"I wasn't going to leave it at that, so I went after her. 'You know fine there's nothing wrong with him. Tell me what it is that you don't like.'

" 'Just something about him, that's all.'

" 'But what?'

" 'Just something. But my opinion doesn't matter, obviously.'

"And she was about to leave the room again when she turned and said: 'All I'll say is that I'm definitely not enamelled.' "

The same fellow-pupil went on to recount that, happily, her mother warmed to her future son-in-law very quickly after that pained first encounter. By the time of the wedding, the two were getting along famously.

"To the day my mother died," she wrote, "she would not hear a bad word said against her son-in-law. He was the son she never had. I sometimes wondered if she preferred him to me.

"There was only one moment of strain in the relationship; when he and I took her off on holiday to Madeira. She was reluctant to go because she had never liked flying, but we persuaded her that modern planes were as smooth as anything.

"After a lot of wheedling, she caved in and agreed to go with us. She even seemed to be looking forward to the flying and began talking about it excitedly for weeks before we went.

"You may be sure that our luck was right out. The flight from

London to Funchal was probably the most violently storm-tossed flight in the history of world aviation. My husband and I seem to have spent half our adult lives in planes, but even we had to admit that it was rough.

"Sickbags were out in almost every row of seats. It's not putting it too strongly to say that at times we were frightened and thought the end was nigh.

"My mother was scared rigid, but it would have been beneath her dignity to admit it. She sat there throughout, hands clamped to the armrests until her knuckles were white. She was staring straight ahead and refusing to speak. I could tell that she was wishing she'd had nothing to do with us.

"We landed safely, if a little haphazardly, and we were just walking across the tarmac to the terminal building when we heard my mother saying:

" 'Thank God I'm back on terra cotta.' "

Someone reminded not long after this column appeared that I wasn't exactly innocent of malapropisms myself.

I was once chairman at the grand final of the Press and Journal schools debating competition, which involved six months of competitive debating among 50 secondary schools from throughout northern Scotland.

At the grand final in the Mitchell Hall of Aberdeen University, I was meant to tell the audience of 600 that whoever won that evening would be treated to a long weekend in London which doubtless would involve a lot of "shopping and sightseeing".

Except I promised them a lot of "sopping and . . ."

44. SWINGING THE LEAD

Or how to perfect the art of malingering

▬▬ ▬▬ ▬▬ ▬▬

*"Always blame diarrhoea, he said, when you were
phoning in sick. The person at the other end of the phone
would be too embarrassed to probe further."*

IT HAS been a tabid week in the howe. As all you ladies
know, one of life's constant truths is that when illness strikes
a man, he soldiers on, stoic and uncomplaining. Indeed,
you'd hardly know there was anything wrong. It's something in
our genes. When illness strikes a woman, everyone knows about
it. (I think that's the right way round.)

I mention this only because Mrs Harper is off school with the flu
at the moment. It's the bug that appears to have done the rounds
in Scotland. It starts as a stomach cramp, progresses to a lashing
sweat and wobbly legs, followed by a burning thirst and
headaches.

We're told it peters out in light-headedness and ravenous
hunger but, as this is a work still in progress, we're not in any
position to confirm.

It's a good thing that I've been working from home for two days.
Between piecing together columns, trying to catch up with a small
mountain of work-related correspondence and preparing for a
new book, I have been answering that croaky, faint: "Hello?" that
drifts along the top landing every half hour or so.

If it's not herbal tea, it's a glass of hot water.

These are the times that most test marital harmony. If the healthy one can put up with the interruptions, and if the ill one can thole the ham-fistedness, relations are probably pretty secure.

I don't mind the frequent calling in the least, for she has done the same for me, and far more often. I'm just not much of a nurse. Thermometers are strangers to me. A poultice is a waste of a good loaf.

I have tried cheering her up with a witty quip or two. I said the other day that all she needed was a few cobwebs and she'd be the spit of Miss Haversham from Great Expectations. That didn't go down terribly well.

But at least her illness is real. In a quarter of a century, I have worked alongside several shameless rogues who have concocted all manner of health-related excuses to swing the lead.

One chap called one December morning to say that the snow in the night had been so bad that he couldn't get his car out, so he wouldn't be in to work. He lived two streets behind Press and Journal HQ.

Another used to complain of a recurring bad back, which mysteriously prevented her sitting at her desk and working, but never seemed to trouble her on the dance floor that same evening.

But for 24-carat cheek, I have to hand it to a former colleague who had shirking down to a science. He moved south almost 15 years ago now, and has lost touch with all his old cronies, so he won't be embarrassed if I reveal his secrets.

It was of this colleague that one former news editor said: "He hasn't had a day's illness in his life. It's always at least a week."

Lesson One was the phone call. To make it sound convincing; to get that croaky quality in the voice, he breathed a kettle's steam for half a minute or so, then took a couple of gulps of cold water and phoned immediately. Alternatively, he said, a heavy blooterment the previous evening did much the same job.

Lesson Two was the complaint. Always blame diarrhoea, he said. The person at the other end, without fail, would be too embarrassed to probe further.

Lesson Three: be prepared to be convincing; visiting the doctor, if necessary.

It was this dedication to his art that brought his finest moment, he said once. Asked to bring a urine sample to the surgery, he had searched his flat for a suitable bottle but, being a bachelor, all he had that fitted the purpose was an empty half-bottle. He rinsed it out and took it to the toilet,

The way he told the subsequent story was much funnier, longer and more involved, but the long and the short of it was that he took a bus to the surgery and left the bottle on the bus by mistake.

He described at great length the other passengers on the bus, and wondered which one of them might have spotted the bottle and slipped it surreptitiously into his coat for later. My only concern is that you had to know this particular man to doubt that he could have left a half-bottle anywhere.

But then, he wasn't married, you see. That was his problem. He had too much time on his hands outside work.

He didn't have that mutual support that helps husbands and wives through their various misfortunes. He didn't know what he was missing.

Or maybe he did.

I've been thinking of one of my favourite husband-wife stories. Most of you will remember the diva of Broadway, Ethel Merman: built like a brick outhouse that had been draped in a black spangly tarpaulin, and with a voice to match. Nobody belted out There's No Business Like Showbusiness quite like her.

You should also remember the actor Ernest Borgnine (Dirty Dozen, Marty, Bad Day at Black Rock), who had features every bit as craggy as Miss Merman's voice.

What you might not know is that they were wed to each other for a few tempestuous years. The entertainment industry is known for stormy marriages, and that one was a tornado.

It was so bad that when Ethel wrote her autobiography shortly before she died, she left a page in the book blank to show what she thought of Ernie.

Anyway, the story goes that Ethel was up for a part in a new Broadway musical. By that stage, she was in her early 60s and the producers were looking for a female lead in her 30s at most.

The whole of Broadway society knew that Ethel was desperate for the part, but the producers had already called her agent and had asked that she be let down gently. But Ethel would have none of it. Even when Ernie told her she was wasting her time, she refused to believe that her name and reputation wouldn't be enough to carry her. She was even prepared to audition with all the other hopefuls which, for a giant like Ethel Merman, was quite a concession.

As she left the New York apartment which she shared with Ernie, there was a humdinger of an argument, and she went to the audition not in the best of tempers.

In the event, she didn't get the part, although the producers did their best to soften the blow by clarting on the flattery with a trowel.

She returned a couple of hours later, and Ernie was still draped across the sofa watching TV.

"Well?" he said.

"They said I had the eyes of a teenager, the smile of a 20-year-old and the legs of a 25-year-old."

"But what about your 65-year-old backside?"

"You were never mentioned."

There's a story doing the rounds of Scottish journalism of a prominent husband-and-wife team. The public seem to think this pair are absolutely devoted to each other, but actually they have what can be termed loosely as an open relationship.

"Don't you mind him chasing after anything in a skirt," one of our mutual friends asked the wife one day.

"Not in the least," she said, "he wouldn't have a clue what to do if he actually managed to catch one."

45. FOLLY OF DESIGNER LABELS

Or how not to succumb to cheap consumerism

━━ ━━ ━━ ━━

"Image elects governments. It can make or break even
major companies. It makes people buy new clothes when
the old ones haven't work out. Image is a science."

I T HAS been an eidoloclastic week in the howe. I met an Irish colleague a few days ago and learned something in conversation which rather took the wind from me. There is a factory in Northern Ireland turning out televisions, video-recorders and a few other lines of electronic goods 24 hours a day. No, that's not the surprise.

The plant, owned by Korea, is exceptionally successful, and exports most of its product throughout Europe, adding a hefty whack every month to the plus side of the UK balance of payments.

You might not be aware of that, because the brand name is not one you'll find in premium high-street stores alongside such global icons as Sony, Toshiba and Grundig.

Nonetheless, these TVs and video-recorders sell well at the value end of the market. Some reach the shops as the own-brand stuff of down-market retail chains. Others bear the manufacturer's own name and are sold through catalogues and in warehouse outlets at the price-conscious end of the trade. They also bring jobs where they are needed.

That's not the surprise, either.

My Irish friend was invited to tour the plant a few months after it opened, accompanied by its crisply pressed public-relations officer.

Along the way, trying to maintain his waning interest as another 400 television tubes clattered along the line, looking astonishingly like the 400 that had gone before, my friend asked some pointless question along the lines of: "Do you never want to get out of the bargain-basement market and into the lucrative premium-price stuff like Sony or Sharp?"

All right, here comes the surprise now.

"Not really," the PR man said. "We make a lot of premium stuff for the big players already. The casings are different from our own-brand stuff. We stick on a different badge. The innards are exactly the same."

My Irish friend said that he stopped his slow stroll while he took in the enormity of what he had just been told.

"So," he said, "when people spend £500 on a 20-inch super-duper Wham-a-Tron, CrispColour-a-gogo, hyperlink set with fastext, PDC, CRG, KLM, NRK, DSO and bar, they're getting one of your £199 TVs in a different case?"

"More or less."

"Do they know?"

"I wouldn't think so. It's not something the big players would advertise, is it?"

Then the PR man said something which is true of so much in modern consumerism. "If the customer is happy with the price, the product and the decision to buy, end of story. Don't forget that image has a value, too."

Image.

It elects Governments. It can make or break even major companies. It decides who will hit the music charts and who won't. It makes people buy new clothes when the old ones haven't worn out. It sells cars every six months to some people. Image is a science.

For its fodder, this science depends on consumers who are sufficiently insecure not to want to be seen to be left behind; who fear becoming social outcasts unless they have the latest everything; who are hungry for labels.

I believe that some even go so far as to wear them, although what possesses anyone to venture outside wearing a jacket with Caterpillar across the back, or a T-shirt bearing the legend DKNY escapes me. Must be a brainstorm.

We're meant to think "stylish" and "cutting-edge" when we see a logo on clothes. We're really thinking "sheep" or, if we're in not quite such a sunny mood, "neep".

It's a well known law of retail economics that for every 1,000 image-conscious sheep, there's one who refuses to play the game. Disproportionate numbers of these people live in northern Scotland, I'm told by people who know about market-research things.

And I'm one.

I doubt very much that advertising or fashion have seduced me into buying anything. You have only to look at me to realise that fashion and I are strangers. We didn't even pass in the night.

You won't catch me wearing a logo. Mrs Harper says you'll be lucky to catch me in a clothes shop, full stop.

Every few weeks, if we happen to be out in daylight, she'll slow the pace as we pass a shoe-shop window or a men's outfitters and say: "Look at that in the far corner. Now, that would really suit you. Will we just go in and see if they have your size?"

She might even have her hand on the doorknob, but I will be walking on down the street already, saying: "I've got a pair of shoes at home."

What is this national compulsion to stap wardrobes and to empty wallets needlessly?

It is perfectly possible to exist without 18 pairs of shoes, 10 suits, four coats and a spare thong. There is little so sad as the person who is a slave to what strangers decree is fashionable.

It's not just clothes. Shortly before Christmas, it became apparent that my mobile phone was about to cry its last. Even on a full charge, it would go dead within an hour. When I visited the store, the assistant diagnosed the problem straight away as a geriatric battery and led me to a wall display of new phones.

I listened to the opening bars of the sales spiel before I interrupted him. "I thought you said it was a dead battery."

He blinked. "Yes."

"So why don't I just buy a new battery?"

His surprise showed clearly that it wasn't something he had even contemplated. "But how long have you had that phone?" he said.

"Nearly five years."

He managed to resist shaking his head, but only just. There was the flicker of a pitying smirk instead. "Well," he said, "we might have a battery for that model, but it's a long shot. I'll need to go up and rummage around in the odds and ends of the deleted stock."

"Fine," I said. "I'll wait."

He did have a battery to fit, as it turned out, and I saved £80. As he rang it up on the till, he explained, by way of lame excuse, that even a year-old phone was regarded as Stone Age these days. Many users changed their phones as a matter of routine every six months "just to be up there".

"Up where?" I said, playing the consumer philistine to the hilt.

So, my Stone Age phone will last for maybe another five years, just as my video-recorder has lasted for 13, our fridge for 16 and one of our TVs for 17. Mrs Harper says that, very shortly, the National Trust for Scotland will want to buy me as a museum piece.

███ ███ ███ ███

The obsession with image is has an effect on the jobs market, too. Mass-market motor manufacturers throughout the UK are shedding jobs as demand for their product diminishes.

Meanwhile, the premium brands, mostly German and Swedish, can hardly cope with demand, and consumers are putting themselves in hock to have the latest models. Image, you see.

46. RITES OF PASSAGE

Or why every new recruit has to endure at least one wind-up

■ ■ ■ ■

*"I'm willing to bet that your principal memory of your first
day at work is of the pranks that the older hands played
on you; your initiation."*

IT HAS been a lusory week in the howe. This morning, I want
you to turn your minds back to the week you began work.
There you stood, fresh-faced, eager, looking forward to your
first pay packet; probably a little apprehensive,

I'm willing to bet, however, that that's not what sticks in your
mind about your first week. Your principal memory is of the
pranks that the older hands played on you; your rite of passage;
your initiation.

Hands up if you suffered some form of physical or mental
indignity in your first week of gainful employ. Hands up if you
were duped into making fools of yourselves.

Just as I suspected.

Most of you.

My own happened nearly 25 years ago on my journalism course,
where the entire year was asked to fan out on to the streets of
Newcastle-upon-Tyne to do what is known in the trade as a vox
pop.

Vox pop — it's short for vox populi (voice of the people) —
involves stopping strangers in the street, introducing yourself as a
representative of the Fourth Estate and asking them a question on
an issue of the day. Some are happy to play along. Others whack

you with their handbag and tell you to mind your own business. It's one of the hazards of the trade.

While the course tutors allocated the other students weighty subjects ranging from the prospect of 24-hour television, to political corruption, to lax criminal sentencing, my brief was to approach women in their early 20s and ask if they would consider going topless.

Yes, I'm serious.

You're ahead of me already, I know. You're thinkng slapped face. You're thinking bawled at and kicked. You're thinking chased and thumped.

You're certainly thinking that anyone in his right mind would have spotted that as a wind-up; would have had a hearty laugh with everybody else, and would have asked what was his real subject.

But remember that I, Mr Green and Trusting, had had a sheltered upbringing in the howe, with respect for seniority and authority dinned into me, and although I was unsettled by the topic, the sense of duty kicked in.

I nodded gravely and trotted off.

I'm told that as soon as the door clicked behind me, the tutors collapsed in mirth, certain that I would chicken out and see sense by the time I reached the end of the road.

I fulfilled the assignment to the letter as it happens, and much against my better judgment.

The Geordie lasses took it in good part. Not a single slapped face. Not even a disgusted glare.

I must have looked so forlorn and embarrassed in my mumbling that all of them took pity on me.

Anyway, I returned to rousing cheers at base.

I'm thinking of new-boy and new-girl pranks this week because I've been hearing from my airline contact of the cantrips and capers that go on with new flight crew.

Not for them the hardy annuals of being sent for a bucket of steam, a left-handed screwdriver, a long stand or a jar of elbow grease.

Neither would they be party to the old rituals of the fish-house, where lassies and women would habitually whip the breeks and pants off any young male recruit and apply liberal quantities of fish dye and brine to places best not dyed yellow and salted.

You wouldn't think it to look at fight attendants as they do their in-flight safety procedures or march up the aisle, smiling and saying: "Tea? Coffee?", but flight crew have a rumbustuous and generally earthy sense of humour.

Among the printable new-recruit rituals is the story of the new steward who was called up to the flight deck by the captain and told that the flaps were stuck. Would he mind going back back to the main door and jumping up and down for two minutes to see if he could free them? He did.

There was the new stewardess who was told to go into the hold to cross-check the cargo manifest with the tag on a body-bag. She was in the middle of checking the tag against her clipboard when the "body" reared up and started shouting.

But my favourite involved the young French steward, new to a British airline and desperate to make his mark. His English was fairly basic. He'd done well at school and he'd passed the airline's English-language exam, but he had a thin grasp of idiom and slang, and that was what his new crew decided was his weak spot.

The captain called him up to the cockpit and told him that he would have to give some very bad news to a passenger.

The young Frenchman looked suitably concerned and serious.

"The passenger had a rare and very valuable hamster in the hold," said the captain. "Unfortunately, the heating coils on that bulkhead have failed and the hamster has died. You'll need to tell him as gently as you can."

Fired with the enthusiasm of youth, the steward went back and crouched down beside the passenger, not knowing that the man was a relative of one of the crew and had agreed to play along in the joke.

"I 'ave very bad news for you," said the steward. "Your 'amster 'as died. We are terribly sorry."

The passenger promptly exploded on cue and demanded compensation. The steward, panicked by the angry reaction, rushed back to the flight deck. The captain said: "Offer him £100."

The steward returned and made the offer, but the passenger, hamming his role to the hilt, refused the offer as an insult and threatened to sue the airline for everything they had. The young Frenchman, back with the captain, was panicking. " 'E says not enough. 'E want more."

"Tell him," said the captain, "that you'll give him £100 and a quick canoodle."

The steward went back to business class, crouched down beside the passenger and whispered. "Ze best I can do is give you a 'undred pounds and a queeck canoodle."

Only when the passenger burst out laughing did the young steward realise he'd been had. Even now, I'm told, not a day passes but he doesn't break out in a cold sweat thinking about his embarrassment. Poor devil.

The ones I can't help wondering about are the other passengers in the same row. Presumably, at the final offer, they were making notes to fly Economy next time.

▬ ▬ ▬ ▬

This one brought a heavy postbag, including admissions from men who had been sent for tins of tartan paint or for a box of left-hand threads.

But my favourite came not from a victim, but from a victim's mother, who said her son had been desperate to become an actor and that she had encouraged him to go off to see the management at HM Theatre, Aberdeen, to seek advice. She hoped it would get it out of his system.

But he came back and said excitedly that he had been given a speaking part in the next production. When she pressed him for details, he admitted that she would find him standing at the top of an aisle calling: "Programmes."

47. SUPPORT SCOTTISH TOURISM

Or why a holiday in your homeland can be just the thing

■■ ■ ■■ ■■

"She guessed that Ireland was plugged 10 times more
frequently in the US media than Scotland was, and that
was bound to account for the tourism difference."

IT HAS been a circumforaneous week in the howe. We did
something a few days ago that no sane and sentient adult
should consider doing: we followed Government advice. I
know, I know, the brain must be softening in middle age, but it
seemed like a perfectly reasonable idea at the time.

Ministers from various departments have been doing their level
best, bless them, to kick-start the tourist industry as foot and
mouth disease appears to be passing its peak. You'll have seen
everyone from John Prescott to Chris Smith leering for the cameras
at various half-deserted attractions, frightening small dogs and
making children hide behind their mothers' coats.

They recognise that tourism is one of the three biggest earners
the UK has and that few parts of the country, particularly in
Scotland, can afford to see it dwindle. Their idea is that while
others get down on their knees and plead with Americans,
Europeans and the Japanese not to worry about foot and mouth,
BSE, haphazard rail services, weather, disastrous service and a
dozen other UK catastrophes, they should persuade the British to
support national tourism by having a holiday at home.

So, that's what we did. We had a holiday in Scotland.

It wasn't so much a holiday; more a weekend away, but it was better than nothing. I'll apologise to every tourist-related business throughout the Press and Journal circulation area now, but we opted for Perthshire and East Lothian. We have nothing against the North and North-east, but we know both pretty well already, and we wanted to see bits that weren't fresh in our memories.

It was clear very quickly that everything politicians and the tourist industry had been saying about the downturn in tourism was true. We went out for dinner near Crieff on the first night. We stood inside the door and said: "We don't have a reservation. Would you have a table for two?" The restaurant manager, a tartan-skirted woman of unremitting gloom, swept an arm at the room behind her. Of more than 20 tables set for dinner, none was occupied. Not one. On a Friday night.

She announced virtually before we had sat down that her takings were 40% lower than last year, and she had a beady glint that suggested she was about to try to make up a substantial chunk of her shortfall from the pockets of the two poor saps who had just ambled into her lair. She showed us to a table.

"Is that mostly because of a downturn in North American tourists?" I said.

"Everybody," she said. "Europeans, English, Irish, everybody. They're just not coming. I can understand the Americans, because they scare off if somebody lights a sparkler in Princes Street, but you'd think that at least the British would know that there's no foot and mouth north of Lanark."

I suggested, somewhat naively, that maybe tourists were staying away for fear of spreading the virus. "Responsible tourists," she mused, as if that was a novel notion she hadn't come across in 30 years in the trade.

The meal was excellent, though; probably because the chef was glad of doing something more challenging than counting his cruets. It was also reasonably priced, which surprised us. We had expected a bill at least £10 higher. Mind you, we had also expected not to be eating in the Mary Celeste, so it wasn't a conventional evening in any respect.

Now you're expecting me to tell you a tale of continued gloom at every tourist attraction we visited, but I can't do that because it wouldn't be true. The farther south we headed, the more foreign accents we heard. At our Saturday lunchstop, 100 Americans on a golfing holiday for competition prizewinners spilled from two coachloads, clearly astounded by the blazing sunshine.

Once they had settled themselves alfresco, I leaned across to the next table and asked them if they were enjoying Scotland. A roar of approval rose from three or four of the nearest tables.

Hadn't they been put off by scaremongering TV footage of burning animals? "Not even an epidemic gets between George and his golf," said one rotund matron. The Americans' view was that if the product was strong enough and promoted sufficiently, even epidemics were surmountable.

The tour leader, a slight young thing from Philadelphia named Linda, said that the pull of golf, for many Americans, was stronger than the heather-and-lochs imagery which Scotland tended to trump up in its limited American advertising. She wondered why the country didn't do more to push the sport which had sold itself already, then sell the rest of the country on the back of that.

She had a point. Affluent America's obsession with golf means that Scotland has potentially what amounts to hours of free advertising every week. It's also the one thing that differentiates Scotland from Ireland and which might help Scotland claw back some of the ground lost to our Hibernian cousins.

Why, I asked Linda, was Ireland's pitching to potential American tourists so successful when all we heard in Scotland was of how fragmented, unsuccessful and under-resourced our own industry was. She said she didn't know anything about the politics of tourism in the British Isles, but she guessed that Ireland was plugged 10 times as frequently as Scotland in the American media, and that was bound to account for much of the difference.

Ireland's comparative success, she said, was largely because the Irish got off their beam ends and worked at the PR and the gladhanding, leading to a lot of valuable and regular free publicity. Scotland, she thought, tended to believe it had to pay for every advertisement, which meant that the promotion budget ran out very quickly, leaving an ominous silence.

I said it was unusual to hear of Scots paying willingly for

something they could have for nothing, and she laughed. At which point the rotund matron leaned across and said that she had been disappointed by only one thing so far. "The weather," she said. I said that all Scots considered 16C and cloudless skies a pretty good national performance.

"It is," she said, "but we get enough of that in Arizona. We come here for rain and lochs and greenery. Sunburn we can get at home."

From there, through Edinburgh to East Lothian, the place was hoaching with tourists. French, Spanish, Oriental, Eastern European. There were so many people standing poring over maps in Princes Street that some of the young locals hardly had room to drop their chewing gum.

At the botanical gardens in Edinburgh, one of Scotland's undersung national glories, the foreigners were easy to pick out on a day when the mercury hit 18C. They were the ones not wearing their parkas and anoraks. They were the ones studying and poking their leather-topped pasta bakes in the Terrace Cafe as if the things were about to explode. They were the ones smiling and saying: "Good Morning", unaware that courtesy isn't recognised as a national custom.

But they were also the ones who had taken the trouble to come here and spend their money. On the basis of seed corn, I hope they were treated properly.

▬ ▬ ▬ ▬

I wish I could say that Scottish tourism's fortunes have improved but, if anything, they have got worse, especially since the terrorist attacks on New York and Washington DC. Alas, all the major factors are outwith the Scots industry's control.

48. CURSES, FOILED AGAIN

Or why the best-laid schemes really do gang aft agley

■■ ■■ ■■ ■■

"He returned a couple of hours later looking decidedly less job-satisfied than he had been on the way out. When the pictures were processed, I discovered why."

IT HAS been an expectorant week in the howe. Two weeks, in fact. When, do you suppose, would be the most convenient time of the year for half a dozen key members of the family to collapse with assorted ailments ranging from flu, to barking coughs, to a twisted knee and almost everything in between?

That's right: when they're staying with Mrs Harper and me for Hogmanay and the New Year.

While some families hire cleaning help over the festive season, and some of the really posh ones bring in caterers or semi-professional entertainers, we should have had a wee crew of paramedics on stand-by in the shed.

Among these 24-hour symphonies of hoasting and spyochering, the only ones enjoying anything half-approaching good health were me and the dog, and even he was beginning to look a little limp about the whiskers come yesterday.

He seemed profoundly confused on several mornings, for there had been so much night-time barking from the bedrooms that he had been scratching at his door for most of the night to get out to play with all the other dogs, wherever they were.

That's the thing about Christmas and New Year. When they work smoothly, they really work. When they don't it can be a real challenge to maintain the spirits and keep the mood festive. It's the stress of all that time off and enjoying yourself that brings people to boiling point and makes them behave in ways which they would never contemplate normally.

How else can we explain the scene outside the John Lewis store in Aberdeen on Christmas Eve, witnessed by myself and Mrs Harper? As we were entering the shop, a fractious child was being dragged outside by a mother who was clearly at the end of her rope.

After a particularly piercing juvenile scream, the mother stopped, shook her offspring into a standing position, bent down and, nose to nose, uttered the most ominous threat she could conjure at that moment:

"If you dinna behave yersel right this minute, Gemma, I'll let Grunnie kiss ye the morn."

Gemma, showing insight beyond her years, duly behaved herself.

We can't be too hard on the young mum. The media paint a picture of family smiles and bonhomie throughout the festive season, but the truth is that it tests the stamina and the temper to an incredible degree.

We hear it all the time in the phone calls we receive at the Press and Journal. How else would we explain the incredibly bad-mannered woman who phoned to complain to one of our features staff that she had been trying a recipe we had printed for oatmeal stuffing and that it had been too dry? Since she was a highly accomplished cook, she said, the recipe had to be wrong.

It turned out, in subsequent testing, that the recipe was perfectly correct and that the woman evidently wasn't the classy chef she imagined herself to be. Yet she was so brusque, snooty and self-confident that we could only conclude she must have been a teacher having difficulty adjusting to real life.

Our other seasonal favourite was the man who phoned a couple of days after New Year and demanded: "I thought that the Press and Journal was supposed to be the North of Scotland's paper."

Our staff member said, yes, we hoped that was the service we provided.

"Then why," he said, pulling himself up to his highest dudgeon, "is there not even the slightest mention of the New Year honours lists in this morning's paper? Eh? tell me that . . . if you can."

"Because," said our staff member, "the New Year honours lists were issued last Friday. The Press and Journal filled its front page and two inside pages with lists, stories, picture and personal reaction three days ago."

There was a silence at the other end of the phone for a moment, but then, with that aplomb of every galoot whose balloon has been burst, but who still cannot bear to admit being wrong, the caller added: "And do you really think I had time to read a newspaper last Friday?"

Lesson One: be absolutely sure of your ground before you start poncing around and making an idiot of yourself.

But just in case you think I'm being too hard on certain elements in the readership, I should explain that even among the vast majority of agreeable, appreciative and helpful readers, things gang aft agley.

One Thursday afternoon in 1988, a calamity befell us regarding a picture which we had arranged with a national public-relations outfit to illustrate a feature we were planning to run on the glories of rummaging in antiques shops. I forget exactly what the problem was, but the result was that the picture could not be taken and transmitted from London in time to make our page deadline.

Pitched back on our own resources, I threw myself at the mercy of the talented people on the Press and Journal picture desk. "All I want," I said, "is a picture inside an antiques shop. It needs to show the shop as an Aladdin's cave of goodies. The more haphazard, the better. If it looked like Cocky Hunter's, that would be the best of the lot."

The picture editor scratched his head and collared a passing photographer to see if he knew of an establishment that fitted such a bill. "I do," said the photographer, "but it's a fair distance away."

"Doesn't matter," said the picture editor. "Crack on and look lively. Norman's in a bit of a bind, and we must all be as helpful to each other in a crisis as we can be, no matter the cost or how much personal inconvenience it might entail for us. We must carry aloft the standard of co-operation, willingness and beneficence, or we're not Press and Journal photographers."

All right, I've maybe dressed that up a bit.

Being a forward-thinker, our photographer called ahead to ask if the shop-owner was prepared to be photographed and to appear in print for 300,000 readers. The owner said, yes, that would be quite all right.

With everything set fair, our photographer bustled past my desk, glowing with job satisfaction and promising exactly the type of picture I needed.

He returned a couple of hours later looking decidedly less job-satisfied than he had been on the way out. When the pictures were processed, I discovered why.

There, in a fine array of glossy 10x8s, was the neatest, tidiest antiques shop in Scotland. I'm not exaggerating if I tell you that it wasn't far short of operating-theatre hygiene and order.

"What happened?" I said. "Where's the Aladdin's cave? Where's the Cocky Hunter effect?"

"Well," the photographer said, "after I phoned him, he decided that if he was appearing in the paper, he'd better tidy up."

I think we had to abandon plan B and explain to an extremely miffed antiques-shop owner why we couldn't use the pictures he had gone to such trouble to help us set up.

Ultimately, I think, we relied on pulling an old and dusty print from our archive; a ploy which rescues us on many testing occasions.

49. 'TIS THE SEASON TO BE JOLLY

Or why hand-made presents are better

"Every single item would have graced any home. Budget permitting, I could have carted off several dozen bits and pieces on the spot and been extremely pleased."

IT HAS been a fictile week in the howe. Maybe you've noticed already, but we're into the crunch shopping season of the year. It was as if someone flicked a switch last Saturday. You could hardly get across a road anywhere for nose-to-tail traffic.

It wasn't unexpected. All the shopkeepers I know tell me that the two Saturdays either side of December 1 every year mark the first noticeable surge of Christmas shopping.

The last Saturday before Christmas Day is the single day when credit cards smoke the most, but the first really big lurch into Christmas spending mode is habitually at either end of the first week of December. This is when the air really begins to fill with the sound of tills ringing and husbands' patience fraying.

At first, I wondered if the timing was psychological. Perhaps the turn of November into December made shoppers realise suddenly how little time was left before Father Christmas was due to set off on his rounds.

But now I know that there is a far more practical reason than that. It's quite simple: most people are paid at the end of the month. With the evidence of the payslip in front of them, people feel more inclined to go out and blow the lot. At least, that's what shopkeepers tell me, and that's why they begin hiring extra staff.

While I'm delighted that shops appear to be doing record business for a change, I'm half-sorry that so many people will be getting the same mass-manufactured stuff for their Christmas gifts. Maybe it's my age, but I've taken an awful hankering for craftwork.

If you think that craftwork means badly crocheted toilet-roll holders done up as regency dolls; pottery pipers glued on a lump of granite, and mirrors with bits of straw and felt and ribbon stuck round the edges to make them look rustic, you've got the wrong idea.

Modern craftwork is as much about design as about workmanship. In all cases, it's immeasurably better than the shop-bought, mass-produced stuff. Each piece is hand-made with a craft worker's care, and it shows. Craftwork needn't be expensive, either.

That much struck me when I was at the Turriff Academy PTA Christmas Fair on Saturday morning. The hall was filled with tremendously accomplished work; most of it done by people who enjoyed their craft just as a hobby. That's the sort of place to buy your Christmas gifts.

Many people in northern Scotland appreciate the fact that personal effort has gone into making something, whether that something is a jumper, an ornament, a carving or a cake.

Be honest, now. Who among you has not taken a first sip of a plate of soup in a cafe, screwed up your nose and whispered to a companion: "Oot o a tin."?

Who among you has not been out visiting, enjoyed a fly cup at your hostess's expense and then, on the way home, observed: "Half that pieces wis shop-bocht."?

Come on, now. Admit it. Every last one of you.

Derision awaits the unwary housewife who can't turn out a batch of scones, and it's just as difficult for the husband who can't put in a decent dreel of tatties. Northern Scotland prizes personal effort and skill.

And that's why we take so enthusiastically to craft fairs. Maybe I'm just catching the craft bug late in life.

The most professional craftsman I came across was at a craft fair on Deeside eight or nine years ago. He was so professional that he didn't have one of those little metal cashboxes or a wee wooden tray to hold his change. He had a battery-powered cash register. How's that for hi-tech?

Anyway, I have a soft spot for good wood-carving, metal sculpture and glasswork, and this multi-talented fellow was a dab hand at all three, judging by the wares on his stand.

You know that feeling when you arrive at a shop for the first time and know immediately that you could blow far more than you could afford on almost anything, given the chance? That's what this man's stall was like.

Every single item would have graced any home. Budget permitting, I could have carted off several dozen bits and pieces on the spot and been extremely pleased. Best of all, like every good craftsman, he hadn't made the mistake of assuming that people would pay shop prices at a country jamboree, and all of his items were tagged fairly, albeit considering the many hours of work that had gone into each one.

I held back while people swarmed round the stall. Between the curious battery rasp of his cash register, he answered questions politely and cheerfully.

He had that sort of set about his face which suggested a good sense of humour, for he was soon twinkling and bantering with all the old ladies, and they were soon dipping into their purses and taking away spurtles, bowls, lampshades and many of the smaller items. The battery-powered cash register was rasping and pinging merrily.

I joined the throng after the first rush was past, and soon there were only two elderly women and me left. The first woman presented the stallholder with, oh, let's say half a dozen items that she had picked to buy: spurtles and trinket trays and a pen pot; that sort of thing.

Between cracking jokes, he began wrapping the woman's purchases and ringing up each on the register. On the third or fourth item, the rasp of the cash register became a growl and a cough, followed by a loud wail.

He cleared the amount and tried once more. The same growl

and cough and whine came again. He flicked the On-Off switched and tried for a third time. Same again.

He apologised for the delay while he went back to his car to get fresh batteries. It took a couple of minutes to replace them and he tried again. This time, success.

"There we go," he said, reaching over his stall to fill his elderly customer's shopping bag with each of her new purchases. "Sorry about that little problem."

"Dinna worry aboot that," she said. "I jist hope I didna damage yer till."

"Don't you fret, my dear," he said. "There's nothing wrong with the till."

"I hope no. I widna like tae think I'd broken it. So, how much am I due ye?"

He tore the paper printout from his cash register. "There you are," he said, "that'll be £462,000, please."

- - - -

The craft worker in question recognised himself in this column and phoned to say that he had given up on his cash register because it was proving far too unreliable and, besides, it struck a discordant note with customers to see this example of modern technology on a table of hand-made goods.

Instead, he said, he had made himself an abacus, which he had intended mostly for show because an abacus wasn't really up to the pace of commerce even at a craft fair.

Then a customer had come along at the next fair he had attended and had demanded to buy the abacus. He had discovered a new sales line quite by accident and was planning to make more.

50. WHEN SCOTLAND'S NOT AT HER BEST

Or how to prepare for an 11-month winter

■■ ■■ ■■ ■■

"Most older families have photographs of an appalling
January-February in the early 1960s when the ploughs
piled up snowbanks on either side of the main road."

IT HAS been an isochimenal week in the howe. If I cast my
mind back to what passed as our summer in these parts last
year, I recall meeting one of my older compatriots in the
village one Saturday afternoon and the two of us drawing the
appalling weather through hand.

We'll call him Alfie, although that's not his real name and, as
you'll see, he deserves to have his identity protected.

Alfie agreed that it was possibly the wettest, worst summer he'd
seen since the early 1960s and, as someone steeped in farming
lore, he'd seen quite a few wet summers. Alfie opined that the cost
of drying whatever grain managed to stand up to the bad weather
would render a whole year's work next to worthless at a time
when farmers could have done with some good news for a
change. As we stood there, cars splashing through the puddles at
our side and their lights reflecting in the gloss of the tarmac, Alfie's
parthian shot was one that has stuck in my mind these last six
months.

"Bit look at the good side, Norman," he said.

Soaked to the bone, it was hard to believe that there was a good
side, but I waited to hear what was sure to be a gem of old
agricultural weather lore.

211

"Mark my words," Alfie said, "wi a summer as weet as this, there'll be nae sna this winter. Dry winters efter weet summers."

"No snow at all?" I said.

"Nae even a flake. Guaranteed."

So, there you go Alfie. I'm looking out at nearly two feet of nae even a flake. I'm looking at a car that has doubled in height thanks to two feet of nae even a flake. For ages now, like everybody else in the howe, I've been digging, re-digging and digging all over again paths through two feet of nae even a flake and, boy, is it sore on the back.

I'll stick with Heather on the Weather in future.

I don't recall many snowfalls as bad as this in my 43 years here. It must be bad; the ITN evening news devoted a whole eight seconds to it as the sixth item in Sunday's bulletin. Had it been Surrey, of course, it would have been the five-minute lead. At least both main channels repaired the misjudgment as the week wore on.

Most of the older families in the village have photographs of an appalling January-February in the early 1960s when the ploughs piled up snowbanks on either side of the main road out to Aberdeen. Judging by the scale of the men and children waving at the camera, the drifts and banks look at least 10ft high.

I'm too young to claim any personal memory of that, but many of my elders and betters remember 1947 and simply shake their heads as if the memory is too painful to recall.

There are also pictures in the Press and Journal archives showing entire trains on the old Buchan and Macduff lines, all but disappeared in snow so deep that they might as well be in tunnels.

Our "Blizzard Pictures" archive draws gasps from most people who see it. There's Union Street in Aberdeen with snowbanks tall enough to hide almost the full depth of the street-level windows at Watt and Grant. From memory, there are pictures of Mid Street, Keith; the Cullen Viaduct, Inverness Station and the centre of Fraserburgh, all looking more like base camp on Everest than towns in northern Scotland.

Incomers, especially, find it hard to believe that winters in North Scotland can be so hard because we've had it relatively easy these last 30 years. According to the records, what we're getting this week is actually the norm.

The archives are also filled with sad tales from throughout the second half of the 20th century. Children who fell through ice while playing and drowned. Teenagers who got lost in blizzards on a two-mile walk home from school. Hillwalkers who disappeared in February and whose bodies were not found until May. Drivers whose cars became stranded and who made the understandable mistake of running the engine to keep warm as the drifts piled higher, only to gas themselves.

When the police and the rescue services advise us to stay put unless travel is absolutely essential, it's maybe as well to remember what can happen and to heed the advice.

Which brings me, trying to inject a much-needed cheerier note, to two tales of blizzard conditions which have become staples of story-telling soirees in northern Scotland. Curiously, both stories hail from Upper Banffshire; from the Cabrach, to be precise.

The first involves a blizzard of a fury and power that the rest of us can only imagine, but which must have been second nature to those hardy billies who eked out their existence on the thin, peaty soil of the Cabrach moors.

If you're familiar with the Cabrach at all, you can well imagine the low stone cottages piled high with drifts blowing unstopped across bare country, and the inhabitants coorieing down inside and hoping for the best.

The first tale has an air of the early 1950s. Allegedly, the police from Huntly and Dufftown had been co-ordinating a check on all the inhabitants of the high country. They had accounted for all but one and called out a rescue team with dogs and sledges.

After a couple of hours of wading through snow the like of which few of them had experienced before, they saw the cottage taking shape from the whiteout. They were surprised to see a light burning merrily in the window, and the fact that paths had been cleared around the house spoke of someone who wasn't about to let snow upset his routine.

The team leader knocked on the door.

Presently, a voice came. "Fa's there?"

"It's the Mountain Rescue."

"Awa ye go. I put thrippence in yer tin doon at the shop last wikk."

The second tale dates from much earlier. This blizzard was shortly before World War I; one of the worst on record. The Cabrach was much busier then, and the community had rallied round to check on each other. Everyone had been accounted for except Jimmy.

A party had set off, roped together, for the three-mile hike to the cottage where Jimmy lived alone. When they arrived, there was nothing save a plume of smoke appearing from the snow. Drifts had buried the cottage completely.

The first crofter clambered across and reached the smoking lum. He lay flat and shouted down: "Jimmy, it's Wullie here. There's fower or five o's. Are ye aaricht?"

"Deein gran," came a faint voice from below.

"We wis thinkin we'd dig ye oot. It's an affa nicht o sna. Blaain like the verra deevil. We'll be as quick's we can. Can ye wyte or we dig ye oot?"

"Dig me oot?" came the reply. "Fit the hell wid I dee oot on a nicht like this?"

▪▪ ▪▪ ▪▪ ▪▪

I have learned from long exprience that weather stories take a trick with the readership almost as much as do items about the Doric, so it's probably just as well that there are two weather-related columns in this book.

Every so often, I make a request for old examples of weather lore. This trebles the volume of mail for about a week, for which I am truly thankful.

51. FROM THE BOTTOM DRAWER

"You come across things which time has rendered puzzling. Other items make you wonder why you deemed them sufficiently important to warrant keeping."

I T HAS been an eclectic week in the howe. We have succumbed to that old Scots habit of our forebears and begun tidying up odds and ends, drawers and presses, so that we may face the new year with an equally tidy conscience.

One of things about sorting out a writer's study is that you come across all manner of things which the passage of time has rendered puzzling. Other items make you wonder why you deemed them sufficiently important first time round to warrant keeping.

Still others — clippings, letters, photographs, hasty scribbles of overheard conversations, and other minor treasure trove — have obviously been waiting for the muse.

It's my habit to hold back certain items until a sufficient collection on a given theme has built up, then I stand a chance of trying to knit them together as a Wednesday column. Not all of them find bedfellows.

Spread before me is a year's worth of odds and ends which, although worth keeping, would never really have sat properly alongside anything else. There are only so many leaps I could make from cinemagoing in the 1960s to the best mealie puddings in Banffshire and back to bus-stop arguments. So they have been lying, waiting patiently, for their time to ripen.

And here it is.

Seeing as it's Christmas, and we're all beginning to wind down from our daily labours and catch our breath in time for the festive season, I thought I'd deliver a bit of a mixter-maxter from my Odds and Ends tray. Many of these tales come from chatty letters from readers, so if you don't find them as entertaining as I do, at least I don't have to take full responsibility.

The first is a letter from a Nairnshire reader, who recounts going with three of her workmates to a cinema in Inverness to see Dr Zhivago in the mid-1960s. Since the national publicity machine of the time had built the movie into the biggest epic since Gone With the Wind, sharp cinema managers had upped their seat prices for the first week.

When she got back to work the following day, an older woman secretary asked if she had done anything special the previous night. "I went to see Dr Zhivago," said our reader. "It cost two bob. Can you believe that?"

"What a waste of money," said the older woman. "Stick with the National Health."

A Brora exile, now in Aberdeen, witnessed a nice line in acerbic putdowns. She was at one of those get-to-know-you dinner parties when her husband's firm had appointed a new managing director. The new man had invited his six senior managers and their partners to dinner at a top city restaurant, to oil the wheels, as it were.

Unfortunately, as with most of these things, one of the managers saw the event as his chance to ingratiate himself and began laying it on to impress the new heid bummer. While his colleagues squirmed uncomfortably, he laid forth about how refreshing it was to see new blood in the firm, and that he was looking forward to working in a new regime, and so on and so on.

He was so garrulous that he was oblivious to the fact that his fawning was holding up the whole meal. Even the new MD was looking a little uncomfortable. While the other managers and their wives were wondering how to rein in Motor Mouth, the new MD's wife stepped in and, in 10 seconds flat, endeared herself to the rest of the company; a regard that was to last for the rest of her time in Aberdeen.

She leaned forward and said: "Mr B—, I believe the waiters want to start bringing in the meal. Will I tell them just to start with you, seeing as you've got your mouth open?"

On my recent visits to bookshops round the North and North-east, I fell into conversations with many bookshop managers, one of whom confided that he frequently found it hard not to smile in the month before Christmas when he was trying to help customers who clearly felt awkward being in a bookshop, but who were desperate to find appropriate Christmas presents.

Two elderly North-east women had appeared at his counter asking for help. He managed to find something appropriate for the first woman, then waited for the request of the second, but she seemed eager to be off. Her chum, as surprised as the manager, called the escapee back.

"Are you nae needin a book, Ina?" said the first woman.

"No, nae the day."

"Fit aboot yer brither? Ye could get him a book for his Christmas."

"Na, na. He's already got a book."

One of my favourite Hollywood stories concerns the late director Frank Capra, who made all those inspiring, small-town Americana movies of the 1930s and 1940s, such as Mr Deeds Goes To Town, It Happened One Night and what happens to be the best movie of all time, bar none, It's A Wonderful Life.

Critics of the time raved about Capra's deft work; his intuitive skill at wringing emotion from an audience, but also leaving their spirits uplifted by the time the credits rolled. They called it The Capra Touch.

The longer all this homage went on, the more irritated the studio writers became, for they never got credit for anything, despite the fact that, without writers, there would have been no Hollywood at all, and certainly no Frank Capra.

The story goes that, one day in the late 1930s, shortly after Capra had picked up another Oscar and the headlines were blaring: "Capra Touch Triumphs Again", the great man turned up at his office to read through a few scripts and discovered several envelopes filled with nothing but bundles of blank typing paper.

Each one bore a scribbled covering letter. "Here you go, Frank. Give this 'the Capra Touch'. Kind regards. The writers."

And that's very close to another favourite theme of mine, those fortunate few whose mind is sufficiently quick to be able to bring braggarts down to size. The tale is probably apocryphal, but it's a beauty, nonetheless.

The story goes that one of Scotland's most arrogant businessmen was invited to make a speech to a gathering of the most senior European bankers and politicians at Gleneagles Hotel. The invitation stoked his ego to bursting proportions, and he became even more unbearable than usual.

He ordered his senior managers to prepare a speech for him, but each draft was unsuitable until, finally, he had one poor blighter up a whole night writing the last version. It was handed to him with literally seconds to spare.

The MD strode up to the stage in the Grand Ballroom, gripped the lectern and began reading. The speech was going down well, with ripples of laughter and mild applause in all the right places. He was loving it. Then, 10 minutes in, he turned from Page 10 to Page 11 to read in large red capitals:

"And now you're on your own."

■■■   ■■■   ■■■   ■■■

Every book, like every series of columns and every filing system, must have a Miscellaneous file for tidying up loose ends. The final column of every year in the Press and Journal is my equivalent.

Other columnists on other papers tell me that short takes, as anecdotal compilations are known in the trade, are among the most popular pieces of all. It must have something to do with the attention span being shorter during the festive season.

52. AND MONY MAY YE SEE

Or why Scots mark the end of an old year and the birth of a new

███ ███ ███ ██

"Ask me to pick my favourite Hogmanay and New Year
and I won't hesitate. It was the end of 1979 and the
beginning of 1980, and it wins by a wide, wide margin."

IT'S no accident that New Year is Scotland's festival. Christmas is still regarded by many Scots of my vintage and older as an English import. Before widespread national broadcasting, Christmas was a service at the kirk. New Year was when we let our hair down and consumed to excess. The two festivals were kept much more distinct than they are today.

That lingers. Many Scots families, mine included, still give their gifts at the end of the year, although that's another custom doomed by the advancing tide of seasonal commercial greed and a generation of modern youngster more concerned by the earliest possible arrival of the latest Playstation than by keeping national tradition.

Tradition is the first foot, the lump of coal and the four-gallon pot of broth kept simmering from teatime on Hogmanay into the wee sma oors and beyond to feed half of the arriving wellwishers and to help sober up the other half.

Tradition is the overcoat with a clink-clink-clink from every available pocket and a few other places besides. It's a community whose most determined wellwishers are still wishing you well on January 6 or 7. It's an arm flung round your shoulder.

Tradition is visitors who turn up two or three times in two or three days because by the time they reach the end of their stint, they can't quite remember who they have visited and who they haven't, so it's always best to be sure and do double duty, rather than risk offence.

Ask me to pick my favourite Hogmanay and New Year and I won't hesitate. It was the end of 1979 and the beginning of 1980. It wins by a wide, wide margin.

Partly, it was because of the weather. If you think this week's snow has been bad, I could show you photographs from the dying days of 1979 which prove that, for a crucial time, all four major roads out of the howe were blocked by 3ft drifts. The minor ones were never really in prospect, anyway.

Result? The rest of the world was cut off from civilisation.

If I hadn't known that the howe's gritting crews were noble, upstanding and dedicated to their job, I'd have sworn that their lack of success was part of some grand social plan. Thus, for the first time in years, the entire community was thrown back on its own resources. No one could get out and, more important, no one could get in.

I could fill several columns with the images that remain with me from Hogmanay 1979, helped by an album of photographs which speak of the enthusiasm of a young journalist who had just bought his first good camera.

I could tell you of the parades of villagers up and down the middle of the main street (because the pavements were all blocked and no traffic was moving, anyway). I could tell you of the knots of people of all ages in almost every road, newsing and laughing throughout the evening and into the morning.

I could tell you of the two village worthies (both still very much hale and hearty) who dressed up as the Ugly Sisters to go first-footing, and who seemed to many to get prettier and prettier as the night and morning wore on.

I could tell you of the superstitious household where it was customary not to risk a year's bad luck by being first-footed by a blond dwarf, so the man of the house, who was admittedly tall and dark, if not exactly handsome, would be dispatched out of the front door at five minutes to midnight and left to stand until the bells had come and gone, whereupon he would knock sharply on the door and be invited in as a prodigal returned from far across the sea.

Shortly before he died two or three years ago, he told me that he had lived in the village all his days yet he had spent almost 40 years seeing in the New Year by standing alone in the freezing cold outside his own front door.

I could tell you of a household which, if not exactly TT, was hardly a temple to John Barleycorn, and where many of the younger first-foots were sufficiently respectful to plunk their half-bottles under the hedge and swap them for bottles of Dazzle and Scotch Cola before ringing the bell and being welcomed inside to wish their good wishes.

It was rumoured, although I could never substantiate it, that the man of the house liked to heed the tradition of the lump of coal being brought in as a gift. Over the course of an evening, he would disappear on several occasions to get a single lump of coal from the coalshed, which made this possibly the only home where the roaring fire was kept roaring not by a healthy coal scuttle, but individually, lump by lump.

It is said that his gait became increasingly unsteady as the evening wore on and, if his wife noticed his breath growing ever more pungent, his eyes becoming ever more glassy and his smile becoming ever more floppy, all thanks to the bottle he had concealed in the coalshed, she was sufficiently generous of spirit to say nothing. Well, not in public.

I could tell you of the younger set, people of a vintage slightly more youthful than I was myself, who thought to dare each other to try increasingly daft stunts.

Had the roads been open, the headlights of the cars entering the village would have picked up the dubious sight of a stark naked, if slightly blootered 19-year-old male perched atop the village memorial fountain waving, and not just with his hands, to passers-by.

They said in the weeks afterwards that several of the younger women in the village (and one or two of the hardier pensioners) had first-footed that particular part of the village centre with incredible dedication that year but, of course, I don't believe a word of it.

Looking through the photographs now of Hogmanay 1979, it's sad to see how many of the village notables who were such a feature of my boyhood are not with us any longer, but their wide grins, their faces captured in mid-song, the amber sparkle in their glasses and the fresh batches of red noses and cheeks appearing, wrapped up warmly, at the door speak of a time that they, and I, enjoyed.

It would be good to think that they're all congregating in a kitchen or a living-room somewhere else, with a host saying: "Ye'll hae a something."

Had they still been around, and perhaps even if the roads block this time round as the old year dies and the new one is born, you can be sure that the clarion of the modern Hogmanay and New Year won't be heard around these parts:

"Fit like wis yer New Year?"

"Och, quiet, ye ken. Quiet."

This one painted perhaps an inaccurate picture of the typical Scottish New Year, as some readers suggested.

The more customary New Year is a pretty dreich affair. January 1 is usually unremittingly drizzly and gloomy, with pretty tired fare on the TV and even ropier cuisine left over from the bits that the previous evening's revellers didn't get round to consuming.

There's also the entertaining possibility that you'll find a stranger snoring behind your sofa.

Write to Norman Harper at:
The Press and Journal,
Lang Stracht,
Mastrick,
Aberdeen
AB15 6DF

Send him an-email at:
n.harper@ajl.co.uk
or
fortnights@stronach.co.uk

Or log on to:
www.stronach.co.uk